GOD'S WILL

DR. GEORGE PETER AMEGIN

authorHOUSE®

AuthorHouse™
1663 Liberty Drive
Bloomington, IN 47403
www.authorhouse.com
Phone: 1 (800) 839-8640

Published by AuthorHouse 04/05/2017

ISBN: 978-1-5246-7123-5 (sc)
ISBN: 978-1-5246-7124-2 (hc)
ISBN: 978-1-5246-7122-8 (e)

Library of Congress Control Number: 2017901985

Print information available on the last page.

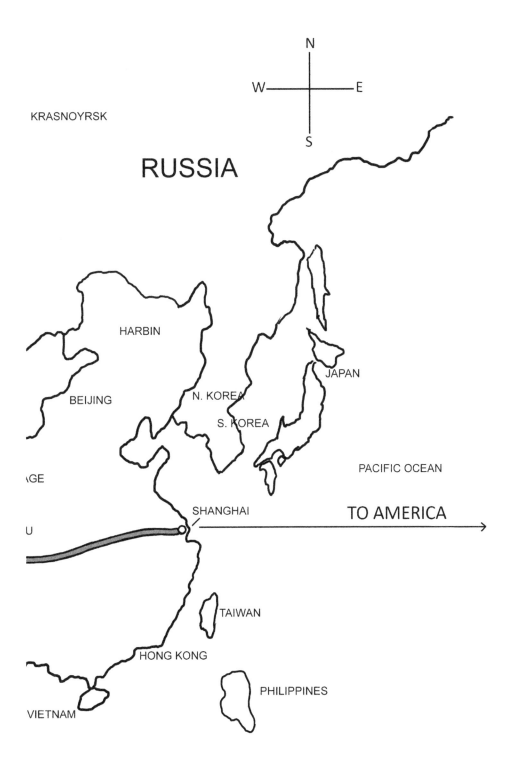

Mrs. Edith (Edie) Adrian (Porter) Amegin
Deceased January 18, 2013
My wife, Mother of my children, Musician, Teacher,
Business Administrator, and a friend to all.

Proceeds from the Book
90 percent of proceeds received from the book sales will go to orphans, elderly, sponsor summer missionary trips and Edinburg Theological Seminary distributed through our non-profit 501C-3 World Healthcare Foundation

www.WorldHealthcare-Foundation.org

Contents

List of Illustrations

Foreword

"A journey of a thousand miles," it is said, "begins with one step," and this is true, but so does the movement of a hamster's wheel. Most of us humans are more like the hamsters: steps upon steps, millions of steps, 'round and 'round the squeaky wheel, ever faster, going nowhere until we plop out the side and another hamster takes over. "Vanity of vanities," says the Preacher, "all is vanity." It is not a modern refrain.

Our heart longs for a real journey—one that transforms the soul— and so we read about it and we write stories: Homer's *Odyssey,* Dante's unforgettable trek ever downward through the seven circles of Hell and onward up to Paradise, *Gulliver's Travels, The Voyage of the Dawn Treader* from Narnia to the edge of the world, Frodo's harrowing journey into Mordor in *The Lord of the Rings.* The heroes in these stories always end up changed, and their authors seek to move us to seek the same change! A few do. Most of us keep running in our wheels and dream.

But occasionally a hamster (er, human) gets a vision or a calling and really does change. His steps *take* him somewhere. His Creator pulls on his heart—sometimes through joy, sometimes through suffering—and he or she finds a direction and a purpose. At the end those people are changed, and the world with them.

They dot the landscape of history, those movers, those who are called and respond. They are small and imperfect, but they *matter.* We see Abram, called by God from the land of the worship of the moon to go to where he knew not. Moses leaves the backside of the desert to rescue a nation of slaves and—for forty years—lead them to freedom. The Wise Men from the East follow the Star to worship the Everlasting

King. Paul travels the whole Roman world to proclaim the Savior he once persecuted. The Pilgrims on the Mayflower faced perils of sea and a wild foreign land (a great many of them dying) to serve the God they loved.

As pastor at Living by Faith Church in McAllen, Texas, it has been my privilege to know one of this kind of man-on-a-journey, and a great honor to be asked to write the foreword to his book. Dr. George Amegin is not an imposing man to look at. The real journeyers often aren't. They're more like hobbits than superheroes, plain folk you probably wouldn't glance at twice on the street. But once you meet them, talk to them, and go past the skin, you find the depth of one whose life has a calling and a direction, and was not lived on the hamster wheel.

The journey he writes about in this book spans generations. It starts with a wrenching family separation born of poverty, hunger, and the deadly cold of Siberian Russia, wends its way through China and finally across troubled seas to the United States. It is a journey of growing faith shaped in the harsh crucible of a world wracked by two world wars, economic upheaval and the rise of the red hammer of communism.

In that crucible the hand of God moves time and time again, touching hearts at just the right moment, causing those "coincidences" which those who pray see so often.

As I read through these pages, I couldn't help but be moved as I watched God mold and shape a family with a patient hand, year after year, testing after trial, into the people I love and respect today. Dr. Amegin has blessed me immensely, both professionally—as an excellent ophthalmologist he has taken care of my very poor eyes—and in ministry, as he has helped Edinburg Theological Seminary where I teach. He also fills our evening worship service with the delightful sound of his trumpet. His daughter Natasha has also been a great joy and inspiration to me and others at the church. It is my hope and prayer that you take your time as you journey through this book. May God touch you, as He did me, with a flame that moves you to leave the wheel behind, and make our own journey matter.

Thomas Whitehouse, Ph.D.

Preface

The story in this book is not about how one man against all odds took his family halfway around the world from Siberia to America. This is about how God reveals his wisdom, power, and knowledge in our present everyday lives!

God plotted a course for this simple man and his family from Siberia to an unknown destination. He led them through the valley of death! He led them through the land where there was war, starvation, disease, imprisonment, torture, and death! All this was simply for refusing to deny Christ and for not accepting communism as the true god of mankind!

God positioned His chosen servants, believers and nonbelievers, along the course of their journey to guide them through the land of war, disease, starvation, and death. Subsequently, He led them to their destination! "The land of milk and honey, America!" Only when we reached America, did God reveal to my father the final destination of his journey!

All the believers in the Russian Baptist Church in the Northwestern Russian Chinese border town of Kuldja, were sure that Amegin (Shelohvostoff) family died fleeing from Kuldja across the war zone! If they didn't get killed in the war zone fleeing from communism, they surely died trying to walk across the Gobi Desert with eight children! By now everybody had forgotten about the Amegin (Shelohvostoff) family. Everybody in the community was sure that they were dead!

About ten months after the family departed, word reached Kuldja that the Amegin family was alive and well! They had reached the coastal city of Shanghai-- all the way across the continent of China!

The church members in Kuldja, said, "If they could do it with no resources and walking, we surely can do it with all the resources that we have!" They started fleeing towards Shanghai to freedom from communism. The window of opportunity was closing rapidly! Many of them did not make it. Those that survived, came to Shanghai almost a year later. By now, all the avenues to freedom from communism were closed off by the communists. Through immigration attorneys in Shanghai many unsuccessful attempts were made by the group to come to America! By now the communists closed all avenues of freedom from China. The group was not allowed to come to America, instead they were sent to Philippine Islands!

Father would not give up! He insisted to the immigration authorities that the group must come to America! This is my flock from Kuldja in Northwestern China and I was their pastor. These are my brothers and sisters in Christ! I must help them to come to America! Father turned to area Russian churches in California to get sponsors and help to bring the group from the Philippines to California! Everywhere he went, he was told that there were too many of them and too few of us. There was no way we could sponsor such a large group halfway around the world! Father did not give up. He said, "I know it can be done!"

With the help of Brother Niedens in San Francisco, and Brother Wolin in Bryte Russian Baptist Church, my father proceeded to work on the monumental task. With the help of my older sister and myself, we traveled monthly and bimonthly to San Francisco, a distance of about 90 miles to work with immigration authorities to prepare the legal paperwork needed to bring the group from Philippines to America!

When and where it is impossible for man, God steps in and makes it possible!!!

Acknowledgments

My most important acknowledgement is to God for allowing me the wonderful privilege of writing this book and capturing only a fraction of a moment in time the power, wisdom, and knowledge of the almighty, living God throughout the universe.

To Edith (Edie) Adrian Porter Amegin, my wife, who died January 18, 2013. After hearing my testimony, she immediately said that I needed to write a book about our persecution by the communists because we were Christians and our flight from them.

To our children, Natasha, Daniel, John Marc, and Peter Guy, and their spouses, children, and grandchildren, for providing strong support, prayers, and encouragement in the writing of this book.

To Bill and Jim Schoerner, Anna Schoerner Loss for providing accurate dates and facts from our association in Lanzhou, China.

To Tava Granchukoff (Shelohvostoff Amegin), who recently died, for verifying all portions of the book as being factual!

To the Granchukoff family, for assisting me in gathering photographs and existing documents!

To Zena Kotko(Granchokoff), for opening her home to me numerous times while I was in Sacramento, California, gathering information from her and many others.

To Dr. Vera Sawicki Granchukoff, for providing the needed name and photo of the last free ship leaving communist Shanghai Harbor.

To the Armenta family (Simon, my daughter Natasha (Amegin), and our grandson Tony Lopez), for technical and computer support.

To Natasha, my daughter, for helping to proofread and edit the book.

To Alex and Donna Amegin, for doing extensive research and providing valuable information for the book.

To Mike and Nida Lokteff, for providing valuable information and photos for the book.

To the Tony Amegin family (Larisa, Danny, Ruthy, and Rita), for their support and for providing needed information!

To Lydia (Amegin) Juedas and the Dale Imhoff family (Nida, Kathy Washburn, Leanne Hickman), for providing photos for the book.

Donna Antoniuk thank you for editing the book.

To the University Eye Center—all four locations—a big appreciation to all my staff for being patient with me and professional, compassionate, and understanding while treating all my patients!

To Dr. Mae Wesson, thank you for your input and helping us run the clinics.

To Diana Mata and Natasha Armenta Amegin, my office managers, thank you so much for managing the offices smoothly, which allowed me to work on the book! Thank you for arranging all my flights and work schedules! Diana, thank you for helping to collect information, photos, and doing all the emails for the book.

To Kenneth and Helen Suk, for verifying information and providing photos.

To Annie and Rick Loncarovich for providing photos and information for the book

To Avijit Mukherjee (Obee) Thank you for being selfless in helping me take care of our patients.

To Sandra Saldana you help during this time is greatly appreciated.

To Rigo Serna, thank you so much for your assistance in obtaining the needed photographs along with the permission to use them.

To Thomas Whitehouse, P.H.D. Thank you for writing the Foreward and for your input.

To J.P. Roberts Haine T.H.D., P.H.D. Thank you for your guidance and valuable input.

My apology to those whom I may have forgotten to mention for your help in writing this book.

Chapter 1

My Grandparents

My grandfather went to work for the railroad in the bitterly cold Siberian region of Russia. One day, a man came to the house from the railroad department and told my grandmother that her husband had died in an accident. He did not tell the details of the accident or why it had happened.

Because she received no benefits from the railroad, she faced the tragic reality that she would have to fend for herself and try to survive the best she could with her two children. Because Grandfather had just started to work for the railroad, they had no money saved up. This and the fact there were no benefits from the railroad meant Grandmother was left penniless with two hungry mouths to feed. The landlord was gracious enough to let them stay in their house rent free until the summer, at which time she would have to start paying rent.

There was, of course, no way she could continue to support the two boys and herself through the freezing cold Siberian winters. She talked to her friends and the church officials to get suggestions and ideas about how she and her children could survive. Her friends and the priests from the church told her that she should take the boys to the monastery where they would be well cared for. There, they assured her, the boys would have a roof over their heads, clothes, food, and most importantly, an education.

As winter set in, my grandmother went back to the church, one more time, to talk to the priests, just to make sure that taking her sons to the monastery was the right thing to do. The priest at the Orthodox church assured her it would indeed be the best step for her to take. He said that they would get a Christian education and might even become priests of the church in her village. The church certainly could use them.

Now, Grandmother, being a very devout Orthodox Christian, believed what the priests told her and soon decided to take the boys to the monastery. Deep inside her heart, she knew that the priests were right. Instead of slow starvation and freezing to death, the boys would have a roof over their heads, clothes on their backs, food, and possible education.

However, after spending many exhausting, sleepless nights and days pondering this life-changing decision, she was no longer sure. The issue remained unanswered. It was frightening and heart-wrenching. While wrestling with her thoughts, she strongly and selfishly became convinced that she could provide for them. The three of them could survive. Then reality would set in once again, and she would envision herself and the boys dying from starvation and cold. She could not bear the thought of losing her boys in such a way.

So with mounting emotional turmoil, physical stress, and mental fatigue, she realized that the time had come to let the boys go, cut the apron strings, and pray that God would guide them on the rest of life's journey. She did not want to part with the boys but had to. It was a very agonizing and painful decision.

Of course, she was like all mothers—she wanted the best for her children. She knew she could not support them any longer. She knew that she could not provide what they needed. However, the monastery would provide them with almost everything that they would ever need.

It broke her heart to make this difficult decision, but it was a matter of life and death. If she made the wrong decision, it would mean death for all three of them. The right decision would mean life for the boys but a broken heart for her. With time, God would heal her broken heart, and her boys would live.

She had made her decision, and it was final. *The monastery it is!* she told herself. *The new home for the boys!* Early the next morning, she got the boys up and gathered the few clothes they had. She tied the clothes into bundles and then bundled up the boys in their coats and hats with ear covers. Then they all put on homemade snowshoes over their own shoes and walked through the snow. They left on a two-day journey in the blistering Siberian cold to the monastery, their new home.

Their mother knew that they had to make it to her friend's house, which would be halfway between their village and the monastery. They could spend the night there with her friend. The next day they would leave early in the morning to make it to the monastery before dark.

They walked all day, following the sleigh tracks. They saw no fences or houses. They only saw trees covered with snow. She thanked God it was a nice day without wind. As evening approached and the darkness set in, their mother said, "Boys, look everywhere for a light in front of us that can be the house of our friend. We are close, so we must look for the light."

Shortly after she said that, the boys spotted a dim light not far ahead of them! They hurriedly made their way to the distant light. Their mother prayed that they had arrived at the right one and not some stranger's house.

As they picked up their pace and headed toward the light ahead of them, the crunching of the frozen cold snow beneath their snowshoes became louder and more pronounced. It was getting dark and harder to see the tracks on the road in front of them. Once they had seen the dim light ahead of them, the boys hadn't bothered to look at the tracks. They knew where they were going. They headed straight for the light in the window.

The boys were younger, stronger, and more energetic than their mother, therefore, they ran ahead! Their mother, being older and slower, lagged behind the boys. She finally caught up with them, walked around them, came to the door, and knocked.

Sure enough, this was her friend's house. The trio entered the house. Her friend greeted them warmly with open arms. She offered them hot tea, cheese, and bread. The tea consisted of hot water and a little splash of milk, basically to color the water because milk was very scarce. As sugar was not available, she added a pinch of salt to the tea to give it flavor.

The boys finished their snacks and got ready for bed. After feeding the boys and putting them to bed, their mother and her friend stayed up a long time to discuss their situation. Their mother told her friend about her husband's death and their financial situation. The friend agreed wholeheartedly with her decision to take the boys to the monastery, where they would be cared for and get an education.

Early the next morning, they rose and were ready for the usual breakfast of hot-water tea. However, in addition to the tea, each person had a bowl of hot buckwheat cereal with butter and a piece of bread and cheese.

Because the mother and her boys wanted to get an early start, they got their things together and left on the second half of the journey to the monastery right after their breakfast. As they were leaving, their friend told them to follow the road with the sleigh tracks. It would lead them to the monastery. She added that they must not stop and rest too long during the day or they would never make it to the monastery by nightfall. If they did not make it to the monastery before dark, they would freeze to death in the snow.

She repeated, "So, remember, don't rest too long when you stop or you will freeze to death standing still! And don't stop too many times to rest. Keep moving, and you should get there by nightfall."

As they walked, the mother emphasized how important it was for them to keep on moving steadily that day. They didn't want to be caught out in the open at night and freeze to death. They must rest briefly and then keep on walking quickly to make it to the monastery before dark.

As evening approached, the darkness rapidly closed in around them. They continued to follow the sleigh tracks in front of them, but the darkness made it difficult to see them. The sky was gray, and the trees, which were covered with snow, looked grayish white. Most of the trees were white birch, which naturally blended into the background. So everything was grayish white—the sky, the trees, and the road.

They followed very closely the only thing they were able to somewhat see—the sleigh tracks in front of them. They knew if they missed the tracks and made a wrong turn, they would probably get lost in the forest and freeze solid by morning. Those thoughts sent chills down their backs. They didn't want to freeze to death. Images of themselves frozen in the woods became firmly engraved in their minds.

As the thought of freezing became very real, it brought new gravity to the phrase "freezing to death." When they had first started off, they had thought this was going to be a fun trip. They would walk, play in the snow, and have a good time. Now they realized how serious it was. With those thoughts constantly swirling in their heads, they made every effort to follow the almost invisible sleigh tracks in the snow-covered trail.

Several times, the boys had to get on their hands and knees to see the sleigh tracks. Occasionally, it was too dark to see them, and they had to kneel down and use their hands to feel where the snow was packed hard to tell which direction the tracks were heading. That is how they stayed on the correct road.

As the evening became darker, the night's temperature continued to drop rapidly. Now it was even colder. They subconsciously picked up their pace and walked more briskly to stay warm and reach their destination as quickly as possible.

1. Photo of my maternal grandparents.

2. Photo of my maternal grandmother many years later.

As they walked briskly and followed the tracks as best they could, their mother said, "Boys, look ahead. Look for a light. Look for any light! It does not matter whether it is the monastery or a private home! We must find shelter in any home or we'll be frozen solid by morning!" It was getting later, darker, and much colder. They had to find shelter soon.

They thought they were getting close to the monastery. Their mother said, "Let's all look for the little light. That little light hangs above a small door of the monastery that people use."

One of the boys said, "Look, Mother, there's a light ahead of us!" They quickened their pace and walked straight toward the light, as their mother prayed that it was the door to the monastery. As they approached the light, they noticed that it was above a bell, and the bell was above a small door. Their mother quickly reached up to the bell and rang it.

As they stood there in front of the door waiting for somebody to open it, the boys noticed that their toes and fingers were getting numb. They were beginning to lose the feeling in them as they stood there. It didn't feel that cold, but in actuality, it was very cold! They were literally beginning to freeze right at the monastery's front door.

Their mother rang the bell again. Nothing happened. Nobody came to the door. Their mother tried to open the door, but the door was locked. Now they were very concerned. The bitter Siberian cold penetrated their clothes and their bodies, causing them to be extremely cold! Their clothes felt like they were frozen solid. Instead of holding the heat in and warming their bodies, it seemed as if the frozen clothes were sucking the heat out of their bodies.

Then the numbness in their hands and feet slowly spread to the other parts of their bodies. They were on the verge of freezing right in front of the door to the monastery. Could it be that they had walked two days in the snow and the cold and had finally reached the monastery only to freeze to death on its doorstep? How tragic! If only somebody would open the door so they could go inside and get warm.

Their mother frantically rang the bell numerous times. Apparently, the monk, who had been in a deep sleep, was suddenly jarred out of his blissful slumber by the annoying, high-pitched ringing of the bell outside. Deeply annoyed by the piercing sound and still half asleep, he rolled out of his bed as he mumbled under his breath. Steadying his gait by holding onto the walls, he slowly made his way to the small entry door and opened the little peephole. Without looking to see who was there, he yelled out with a loud raspy voice, "What do you want?"

Mother replied, "The priest at the Orthodox church in our village strongly recommended that I bring my boys to the monastery to live, to study the Bible, and to learn about God!" In a moment, the monk unlatched the small old door. The door squeaked on its hinges as he opened it to let them in. They were enveloped in warmth as they stepped inside the monastery. Once inside, the boys immediately sensed the feeling in their fingers and toes coming back.

With an unsteady, wobbling gait, the monk took them to a room where he boiled some water. Soon they were enjoying hot tea, bread, and cheese. After finishing their refreshments, mother explained more about why they were there. She told the monk that she had discussed this with the church officials in her village, and they strongly recommended that she bring the boys to the monastery.

The monk nodded his head in understanding and said, "You made the right decision. You can leave the boys here. We will take good care of them here. They will always have food, clothes, and education. They may even want to become a monk or a priest. One of the boys may even be the future priest in the church in your village. We will help them, and we will educate them here. Here we will teach them about the church and the Bible." The monk then took the boys to a room and showed their mother to a guest room.

Chapter 2

Life in the Monastery

The next morning, everyone was up early. The monks had already prepared a breakfast of hot tea with milk, bread, cheese, and hot buckwheat cereal.

After finishing her breakfast with the boys and the monks, their mother gave each one of the boys a big hug and a kiss. With tears in her eyes, she hugged them again and said good-bye as she walked back through the door they had come through the previous night. The monk led their mother out the same small, squeaky old door. The boys and the monk stood in the doorway and watched as the boys' mother slowly walked away from the monastery and disappeared over the snow-covered horizon. As the boys stood in the doorway and gazed in the direction their mother had gone, little did they realize that this was the last time they would ever see her.

The months slowly passed by. One day as the boys were doing their chores in the monastery, they noticed a stranger coming into the monastery. The stranger did not stay very long. He apparently had some business with the monks, which he discussed briefly, and then left.

Several weeks later, the monks informed the boys that their mother had been found frozen to death on the road back to their village. The monks told the boys that they had no known relatives now that their mother was gone. Henceforth, they would be considered orphans. They would live in the monastery until they were grown up.

Since their first day in the monastery, the monks taught the boys many rules and regulations they were to obey. Everyone had responsibilities, and each person had to do his share of work. A monk assured them, "We will discuss your schedules after you get settled in your new home." They anxiously waited to hear about their schedules—especially the part of the routine where they would be studying the Bible like their mother had told them they would be.

Instead, the monks gave them daily cleaning responsibilities. They were to keep the rooms clean and presentable at all times. They would soon find out that clean and presentable at all times meant scrubbing the floors, the doors, the windows, the walls and washing clothes every day. A monk chided them, "You have no time for play."

Sundays were supposedly reserved for church and Bible study, but they soon discovered that it did not always work out that way. After church, the monks always demanded them to do other chores. The boys had very little time to study the Bible.

Later on, the monks told the boys that Bible study would be done only on special occasions and only if they did all of their chores properly. Their reward would be time for Bible study on Sundays only.

The boys did not think this was right. This is not what their mother had told them they would be doing in the monastery. She had told them they would be studying the Bible all the time, so they thought they would be studying the Bible every night.

The boys worked hard and tried to keep up with all of their daily responsibilities. Some days the chores were so overwhelming they did not complete some of the tasks by the end of the day. The monks punished them for not completing their daily tasks. They told the boys they had to learn how to work faster and harder in order to complete their daily tasks.

The boys did work harder and faster to complete their daily responsibilities so they would have time for Bible study. Studying the Bible was the most important thing to them. They thought studying the Bible was the reason they were in the monastery—to learn about the Bible and God.

With the arrival of springtime, the pair learned they had much more work to do. It was a time for getting the soil ready for planting the garden. When the crops were ready, they had to harvest them and prepare them for winter.

Summertime was hardest on the boys. They had to work longer hours to keep up with their daily chores and the garden too. By the end of the day, their hands were full of blisters, and they were exhausted. They barely had enough energy to drag themselves to their room and fall asleep.

Often, the monks told them they had done a poor job cleaning the rooms in the monastery. They forced them to clean all the rooms again. It didn't matter if it took them all night! They still had to complete the re-cleaning of the monastery.

During the night, the monks began to come in, one by one, and take one of the boys with them to another room. There they would force the boys to have sex with them. This happened several times to both of them. Then it became more frequent. Every night or every other night, the monks forced them to go to the other room and to perform sex acts with them.

The monks strongly advised them not to say anything about this to anybody. The monks threatened them, "If you mention it, you will be punished severely and possibly thrown out in the snow where you will freeze to death! Besides, who would people believe, a couple of incorrigible orphans or the monks?"

Their life in the monastery was nothing like what their mother had described to them. She had told them that they would spend every day learning about the Bible and God. They soon learned, however, that life in the monastery was just the opposite. They found out that life in the monastery was hard work, punishment, and abuse.

As things got worse in the monastery, the boys realized that they were slaves. That's when they began to dream of running away. But where would they go? They had no family and no friends. They were afraid to return to their home village as runaways because people would catch them and bring them back to the monastery. However, they were willing to go anywhere to escape the abusive environment in which they were living.

Chapter 3

Escape from the Monastery

One night when all the monks were asleep and the boys knew that no one was watching them, they snuck out of their room. They crept on their hands and knees very slowly and quietly along narrow, dark, cold, and musty corridors as they made their way to the small side door where they had first entered the monastery. Upon reaching the door, they paused for a moment before going through it.

Mixed emotions flooded their already confused and troubled minds. They broke out in cold sweat from fear. They realized that this was the moment of truth. Freedom was on the other side of that door. If they went back now, the monks might catch and severely punish them for trying to run away from the monastery. If they ran away and were caught and brought back to the monastery, the monks would punish them even more severely. If they tried to explain why they had run away, nobody would believe them. It would be just as the monks had said. People would believe the monks and not the two incorrigible runaways. Then they would be in bigger trouble than ever.

They had decided to run away from the monastery several weeks before this day, and now the time had come for them to follow through with their plan. The doorway to freedom was in front of them. At that moment, they had to make a dreaded decision. Fear and doubt overwhelmed them as all sorts of confusing thoughts came into their minds, which made them very nervous and afraid to go forward through the door.

"Maybe this was not a very good idea," they whispered to each other as they sat in darkness by the door, shivering and sweating from fear. One of them would grab the door handle but would be afraid to open it. Then he would immediately let go of the handle and sit back, leaving the door closed. The other brother would repeat the process again without opening the door. They feared that the door would squeak when they opened it, waking the monks. Now they were more fearful they would be found out. The pressure was mounting.

Instinctively, both boys grabbed the door handle at the same time and slowly pulled the door open. To their great relief, the door did not squeak as it had when they had first entered the monastery. Several days before their planned escape, they had placed butter on all the hinges of the doors they would be going through. They knew that if they had asked for oil or grease, the monks would have been suspicious, so they saved their butter after each meal and greased all the door hinges with it, thereby keeping the doors from making any squeaky sounds during their escape.

As they opened the door, they expected it to be pitch black outside, but to their surprise, the moon was very bright that night. There was also the dim little light above the small door. It was still on, just as it had been when they had first arrived. With it, there was just enough light for them to sneak out and run into the dense forest that surrounded the monastery. In the forest, no one would find them. There, they would be very safe. The forest had plenty of wild berries for them to eat and to survive on for a long time.

After walking all night and then hiding for several days and nights in the woods, the boys were sure that no one was following them. They felt more relaxed in the woods and survived by eating the plentiful wild berries.

The pair decided to take a chance and walk for several days on a dirt path that they came across in the woods. This path led to a small village. As they approached the village that evening, they heard wonderful singing coming from a building close by. One of the boys, who was my father, was very intrigued by the sound. He approached the small building from which the singing came and said, "Let's go in and listen to them sing!"

His brother replied, "No. We can't go in there!" Then without saying another word, his brother turned around and walked away. They were separated there, and my father never saw his brother again. He looked for him many times but without success. It is important to point out that several years after my father passed away, we were able to locate his brother in Russia with the help of Red Cross.

As the boy approached the house, the singing became clearer and more beautiful. It almost hypnotized him. It was as if he was in a trance as he listened to the marvelous music. He felt as if he was in heaven. Then he remembered what his mother had told them about how wonderful it was going to be in the monastery. She had said they would hear beautiful singing all the time, study the Bible every day, and be close to God. All of these memories kept racing through his mind as he stood in the shadows listening to the heavenly music coming from the building.

Suddenly a thought struck him. *Maybe mother took us to the wrong place. The monastery where we were was not like this. We ran away from there because they were abusing us and using us as slaves. They did not teach us about God!*

As he stood there in the shadow of the building, he felt as if he was being drawn toward the singing by an invisible, irresistible force. Yet he was afraid to go in. Why hadn't his brother wanted to go inside? All these doubts and questions swirled within his head. This confused him and kept him from going inside.

He feared all the people. He was sure they would recognize him as a runaway from the monastery. They would catch him and take him back there by force. He shuddered at the thought of going back to the monastery where they would beat and torture him for running away and continue to abuse him as they had before.

Suddenly, his thoughts were interrupted. The singing had stopped, and in its place he heard many happy voices and laughter as the people made their way out of the building. He quickly retreated into the bushes and went deeper into the shadows of the night.

The fear of being seen and recognized grew stronger and stronger within him. He thought his brother might have been right. He should not go in there. It was too dangerous. These last thoughts made him feel sure that somebody would recognize him as a runaway from the monastery. They would catch him and take him back. *I don't want to go back to the monastery! That is the last place I want to go!* he thought.

With these frightening thoughts swirling in his head, he had quickly disappeared into the shadows of the night. The fear of being recognized, caught, humiliated, and sent back to the monastery overwhelmed him. He wanted to get away from all those people that he feared so much.

Blindly he ran deeper into the forest as if by running, he would be able to lose the confusing thoughts that were troubling him. He ran further and further, seeking refuge, peace, and rest. As he ran, all of these troubling thoughts clouded his mind even more.

He tried to satisfy his loneliness and despair in the peaceful, dense, dark forest. There the evergreens seemed to stretch silently and endlessly into heaven itself. Contentment and peace came over his body as his gaze followed the evergreens skyward up to heaven.

The rest of the night, he wandered aimlessly looking for his brother, without success. He then began to search for a friendly, kind, or understanding face of a person who would listen and help him with his very powerful, confusing, emotional burden.

When the morning dawned, he did not know how far or in what direction he had walked. By sunup, he was freezing. He was huddled in a corner between two buildings, which had protected him from the strong, cold, night wind. He had probably wandered into a town during the night and had stumbled into this corner. When his body had felt the protection of the walls on either side of him, he had felt secure, relaxed.

It had felt so good that he had wanted to lean back and rest for a few more moments before going on. He had done more than rest for a few moments—he had fallen asleep while standing in the corner between the two walls. By daybreak, there were all kinds of people with wagons, horses, and chickens. There were also people carrying fresh vegetables. These people were coming and going in every direction. Everybody ignored him as he stood there in the corner. Perhaps they thought he was part of the milling crowd, which had gathered for the bazaar.

Chapter 4

The Farmer's Invitation

Father stood there in the corner between the two buildings and tried to stay warm by absorbing the early morning rays from the sun. He was cold, hungry, tired, dirty, and confused. Just as he was thinking about how hungry he was, a man approached him and said, "Son, if you'll watch my horses and my wagon, I will go and get some hot food for both of us."

Hot food! *This is too good to be true*, he thought to himself. This offer was too good to resist. "Yes! I will watch your horses and your wagon." He didn't need to think twice. He had no place to go. Besides, he was starving. Hot food was what he needed. The food would warm him up and would give him energy and a new outlook on life. Just thinking about the hot food immediately perked him up mentally, physically, and spiritually. Somebody actually cared about him.

This man had given him a responsibility. Wow! Now he felt good about himself. He was somebody important. He wanted to please the man and to help him in any way he could for being so kind to him. He looked at the horses and the wagon. He walked around them and acted like he was the owner's son as he inspected them.

Shortly after that, the man came back with some hot milk and a *piroshki* (a hamburger patty, cabbage, and mashed potatoes, which were all seasoned, or a combination of hamburger with potatoes or cabbage with hamburger wrapped in fried or baked dough) for both of them.

The man offered the food to the boy. He prayed and gave thanks to God for sending the young lad to watch the wagon and the horses. He also thanked God for the food. After he had prayed, they both sat down in the wagon and ate their food.

The rest of the day, the boy stayed with the man and helped him with his wagon and horses. The man had many sacks of corn and wheat in his wagon. He told my father that he must sell these to get money to buy clothes for himself and his wife. By the end of the day, the man was able to sell all of his corn and wheat. He was very happy.

Toward the end of the day, the man asked the boy, "Do you have a place to stay? Do you have a home? Do you have a family?"

The boy responded, "No. My father was killed in a railroad accident. My mother died shortly after that."

"Do you have any friends?"

My father answered no to all of these questions. Then the man asked my father if he would like to come and live with them on the farm.

Father replied, "Yes. I would like that very much!"

The man said, "You could live with us and help us on the farm. I will teach you everything you need to know about farming and surviving. I will teach you how to repair farm tools, how to repair pots and pans, and how to make tools that we need and use on the farm. I will also teach you how to repair guns.

"On the farm, guns are very important. We have many wild animals here. They attack our chickens and pigs and sometimes even kill our cows. Therefore, you must know everything about all the tools that we use on the farm and know how to repair them! You must know how to take care of your horses as well. I will teach you how to do all of these things, especially how to take care of and fix your guns. Without guns it is very difficult to survive on a farm.

"I will teach you how to repair and make wagons and wagon wheels. You will learn how to shoe horses. You will know how to work a farm by yourself if you have to and when the time comes. I will teach you how to provide for yourself and for your future family."

The boy was a quick learner. He was very thankful to the farmer for taking the time to teach him all the necessary skills for making and repairing tools and guns. He learned everything that the farmer taught him. He became very knowledgeable and skillful in all of the things the farmer showed him to do and to make.

Father was very impressed with the farmer and his wife. He helped them to do all the farm chores every day. On Sundays, they always went to church. Father noticed that they always prayed and thanked God for their meals and for their productive days, whether it had really been productive or not. They always thanked God in prayer for everything.

The farmer and his wife told Father that they were evangelical Baptists and not Orthodox.

"We do not believe in the Orthodox beliefs. We do not have monasteries. We have churches where we meet and praise God for everything we have. We especially thank God for His son, who came and died for our sins so that we may have eternal life! It says in John 3:16, 'For God so loved the world, that he gave his only begotten Son, that whoever believes in him should not perish but have everlasting life.'"

The boy was very happy that the farmer and his wife were helping him study the Bible so he would know more about God. They had a Bible, which they shared with him. They also taught him how to read and to write. He continued to go to church with them and would study the Bible regularly every evening after helping the farmer with his chores.

Chapter 5

Accepting Christ

When my father was a young man, he accepted Christ as his personal savior, was baptized, and became a youth pastor in the small Siberian country church where the farmer had so providentially led him. From the start, he showed a strong desire to preach and to evangelize the whole world, just like it says in Acts 1:8, "For you shall receive power when the Holy Ghost shall come upon you and you shall be witnesses unto me in Jerusalem, Judea, Samaria, and the uttermost parts of the earth"

The young man thanked the farmer and his wife for taking him in and teaching him how to live and to survive. Most of all, he greatly appreciated the way they had shared and helped him understand the Bible and his responsibility of spreading the Good News to all the world.

At this point in his young life, however, the young man was restless and anxious. He wanted to go and preach the Gospel. He had a strong desire to tell others about the plan of salvation for all people through our Lord Jesus Christ, the Son of the living God.

The young man said goodbye, thanked the farmer and his wife, once again, for taking him in and educating him in the Word of God, and set out on foot for the next village to preach the gospel. He went from one small village to another, preaching. Sometimes, he would spend two or three days to a week in a village preaching and teaching the Bible.

Once, the young man spent more than a week in a certain village, teaching and preaching the Gospel. After the last service ended on that Sunday, he was getting ready to go to the next village when some of the deacons of the church approached him. They suggested that he go and preach in the smaller villages of Siberia where the communists had not yet penetrated. It would be much safer for him to preach in those remote villages. He took their advice and continued to walk across the southern Siberian countryside, preaching and teaching the Bible to people in the smaller villages.

Chapter 6

Father Meets Mr. Kazakoff

During his travels among the small villages in the southern Province of Siberia, my father, who was still a young man, preached in a small village north of Tomsk. There he met an older gentleman, who was also on fire for the Lord. This man, Mr. Kazakoff, had a wife and two sons.

Mr. Kazakoff invited the young preacher to his home in the larger village of Tomsk, which was about seventy-five miles south of the small settlement where they were preaching the Word of God. The young preacher spent two weeks with Mr. Kazakoff and his family in their home. He appreciated the family's deep commitment and devotion to serve God.

Father later found out that Mr. Kazakoff had been a very wealthy Russian explorer who had accepted Christ as his personal savior and had dedicated his life to serving Him. The decision to leave his lucrative profession and to serve Christ had been a family one. His wife and his two sons had praised and had strongly supported him in his decision to follow Christ. He had left his profession as an explorer and had devoted his life to spreading the Gospel across the province of Siberia as well as other parts of Russia.

The young preacher and Mr. Kazakoff taught and preached the Gospel to the Russian people in the southern province of Siberia and in southern Russia. Many times they were caught and imprisoned. They only escaped with the help of church members in that small village where they were preaching and teaching the Bible.

They became very well-known. The communists knew that my father and Mr. Kazakoff preached against communism. They made every effort to catch and to silence them one way or another. Somehow with God's help and the help of the church members in the small villages where they preached, they were able to stay one step ahead of the communists as they traveled to teach and preach the gospel. They continued to crisscross the country as they headed northwest and deeper into the Siberian wilderness. The preachers tried to avoid them by ministering in the smaller villages where there was no communist presence.

Mr. Kazakoff was an older and more experienced Christian when it came to fighting the communists. He told my father he felt that something big was going to happen in their country.

He said, "I feared for my family! Therefore, I sent them away. I had been thinking about this for a very long time. I sent my family to Los Angeles, California, in America. I have some close friends in Los Angeles who will help my family. My wife and my two sons will be safer there than here.

"I have already made all the proper arrangements for them to be received in Los Angeles upon their arrival there this week. This is basically about four weeks from the time they left here. I do not have to fear for their safety. The communists cannot hurt my family in America. Now that my family is out of communist reach, I can continue preaching the gospel more freely."

The young preacher and Mr. Kazakoff continued to preach the gospel in the province of Siberia and southern Russia with the communists in hot pursuit. They seemed to be one step ahead of the communists at all times, until one Sunday morning when the communists caught them as they were leaving a worship service in a small remote village in Siberia.

The communists told the church members that they were taking them to be questioned about certain matters of preaching. The communists said that after they clarified certain matters they would release them. They wanted to know who was encouraging the young preacher and Mr. Kazakoff to preach against communism and who was paying for their food and travel expenses. The young preacher and Mr. Kazakoff knew better, however. They knew that they would be taken to prison or would be killed for preaching the Word of God.

The communists were convinced that communism was the true god. There was no other god but communism. They thought, *How can Christians go around preaching about a God who is not visible and probably does not exist except in the imaginary, fairy-tale world?* Everybody knew about communism and accepted it as truth. Why were these men so different? Why didn't they want to believe in communism? Communism was the future for all people. It was the *Utopia* for all the masses. How could they not believe in it?

The young preacher told them that no one was paying them. He said that they were ministers and preached the Bible to the people as God had commanded them to. The communists did not believe them. They said that they had to take them to their headquarters in the next village and question them in more depth.

With that, they placed them into a wagon with two armed soldiers and rode off. One soldier was driving the wagon, and the other soldier was guarding the young preacher and Mr. Kazakoff! The young preacher knew that part of the country quite well. He knew there weren't any larger villages in that whole area and there wasn't a communist headquarters in the next village.

The next village was much smaller and there was nothing there. The young preacher and Mr. Kazakoff knew that the soldiers were not telling them the truth. They had just preached in that village a few weeks ago. Besides, the small village that they were talking about was in the opposite direction. They were going away from the village and not toward it.

The communists were taking them into the most remote area of the Siberian wilderness. This was a very desolate area of Russia. They rode deeper and deeper into the dark forest and headed west and somewhat north. One of the soldiers commented that they were going to take them to a special prison. When the time came, they would transport them from that prison to headquarters, where they would interrogate them and get the truth. The young preacher knew that was a lie. There were no prisons in that part of the country. There was nothing there except the wilderness.

As they rode deeper into the forest, one of the soldiers remarked that no one had ever escaped from this prison. The young preacher and Mr. Kazakoff immediately understood that they were going to be executed and dumped deep in the forest where nobody would ever find their bodies. After their execution, they would be dumped in that remote wilderness where the wild animals would devour their bodies in a matter of days, leaving no trace of them in the forest.

The two men knew they were going to be killed very soon. Nobody would ever know what had happened to them. The communists, as usual, would make up a story of how they were questioned at headquarters and were released. The communists would say that they were preaching in the next village. That way nobody would be suspicious and nobody would start looking for them.

As the young preacher and Mr. Kazakoff sat behind the two soldiers, they glanced at each other. Without warning, they jumped and pushed the two soldiers forward and down off the wagon behind the galloping horses. The soldiers instantly found themselves dangling upside down and clinging tightly to the wagon and the horses' reins. Their heads and bodies precariously hung only inches above the ground as the wagon wheels rolled directly behind their heads and the sharp hind hoofs of the galloping horses were inches away from their faces.

The two soldiers instinctively struggled to save their lives. They tried to crawl back into the wagon without being trampled to death by the horses' sharp hooves. They feared that the wagon wheels would run over them. They could hang onto the reins and be dragged and trampled to death; let go of the reins and instantly be run over by the wagon wheels; or quickly let go of the reins, grab the front of the wagon before the wheels ran them over, and climb on top.

Before the soldiers did any of these things, the young preacher and Mr. Kazakoff jumped out of the wagon and ran as quickly as they could toward the dense forest ahead of them. The soldiers regained their positions in the wagon. They picked up their rifles and fired in the direction the young preacher and Mr. Kazakoff were running.

As they ran, the young preacher and Mr. Kazakoff heard the bullets flying by close to their heads. Blindly and frantically, they ran toward the forest to distance themselves from the soldiers in the wagon, who were firing at them. They ran faster when they heard more shots being fired and more bullets flying by close to their heads. As the bullets whizzed past their heads, they became even more fearful and ran blindly, faster and faster toward the more dense forest ahead of them. The young preacher and Mr. Kazakoff knew that if they could make it into the dense forest ahead of them, they would be safe.

The sun was setting fast. The darkness was like a heavy cloud slowly settling over the forest ahead of them and the entire countryside. The problem was that it was not dark enough to hide them from the pursuing soldiers. They were still exposed and in danger of being shot and possibly killed. They ran and desperately tried to reach the cover of the forest and the darkness it afforded. There they would find refuge and rest from the pursuing soldiers.

As they came closer and closer to the trees ahead of them, more gunfire erupted from the direction of the wagon. More and more bullets whizzed by, dangerously close to their heads. Ignoring the sounds of gunfire and bullets, they continued to run. Several more shots rang out, and they young preacher felt one of the bullets barely missed his ear. He looked up and saw that the forest was very near. They would be safe if they could only reach it.

Running as fast as their legs could carry them, they pushed through the thick underbrush and jumped over broken branches and old logs. They stumbled, fell, got up, and ran as fast as they could again, trying their best to get away from the pursuing soldiers.

Now the soldiers fired more rounds in their direction. More and more bullets whizzed past their heads. Mr. Kazakoff, who ran next to the young preacher, suddenly stumbled and fell facedown. He lay there motionless, bleeding profusely from a head wound. Apparently, one of the bullets had struck him directly in the back of his head. It had been a fatal shot.

At once, the young preacher knelt down, looked at him, and realized that the large wound to the back of his head had killed him. Knowing there was nothing he could do for Mr. Kazakoff, the young preacher quickly got up and kept on running, always keeping his head down to protect the back of his head from being struck.

Darkness finally settled on the forest, making it hard to see anything. The young preacher knew this gave him an advantage. The forest was so dark he could hardly see his hand in front of him. He thanked God for this beautiful darkness that had probably saved his life.

Although he knew the soldiers would not chase him through the dark forest at night, he kept on running as quickly as he could. He did not hear any more shots being fired or feel any more bullets flying past his head. He knew he was out of their range of fire. However, he pressed forward relentlessly into the dark forest, wanting to distance himself from the pursuing soldiers as much as possible while he still had the chance. He knew that if he stopped, even for a moment, the soldiers could catch up to him and kill him.

He was dehydrated, drained of energy, and completely exhausted. His lungs not only felt like they were burning from exertion and exhaustion but also felt like they were on fire. He knew that in spite of his total exhaustion, he must continue to go deeper and deeper into the forest to elude the pursuing soldiers. If they found him, they would kill him just as they had killed Mr. Kazakoff.

While desperately running for his life, he gained his second wind, which gave him more strength to continue moving through the dense forest. In spite of his second wind, his lungs, more than ever, felt like they were burning, on fire, and ready to explode.

Frantically gasping for air, he finally reached the point of complete exhaustion and collapsed onto the ground. As he lay there panting, he raised his head slightly and with great effort to see what was around him. Through the darkness, he could make out the form of a big tree in front of him. He decided to crawl over to the tree, lean against it, and rest for a little while.

The forest was now very quiet—not a sound could be heard. He was so exhausted, he fell asleep in a sitting position against the tree. He did not wake up until early the next morning.

Chapter 7

Hiding and Surviving in the Forest

In the stillness of the early hours of the next morning, my father, the preacher, awoke in the forest, which was very beautiful and peaceful. Even though he was still exhausted from fleeing the communists, he felt very weak and hungry.

He got up off the ground and looked for wild berries, which were plentiful and very nutritious. He found lots of blackberries, raspberries, blueberries, and many other kinds of wild berries. After eating enough berries to satisfy his hunger, he again found a nice secluded place, sat down, and fell asleep.

The preacher hid in the forest for four weeks before he had enough courage to approach a village. He feared the communists. He knew that they were looking for him everywhere in order to kill him. Without a doubt, if they caught him again, they would kill him immediately. They had killed Mr. Kazakoff, who had been a devout follower of Christ. He kept telling himself that he must not be captured. If the communists killed him, who would spread God's Word in that area? That struck fear into his heart.

Realizing that the communists were everywhere, Father went ever deeper into the southwestern part of the Siberian wilderness to escape being captured and killed. For several days he headed north, then drifted northwest, and then west, before heading south, and eventually southeast, all in order to avoid the communists. During the four weeks he walked through and hid in the wilderness, he traveled in a big circle through the uninhabited portion of southwestern Siberia. Now he headed back into the region where there were small settlements.

As he continued walking and getting closer to the small villages, he still was very fearful of the communists. He knew that he was on their priority list to be captured and executed. He knew they were very angry that he had been able to elude them all this time.

The Holy Spirit, however, was stronger than his fear of the communists. After surviving in the forest for four weeks, he decided to enter a very small, remote village close to the forest. As he walked all the way around the tiny village, he realized that there were only about ten houses. He did not see red flags on any of them. He didn't think the communists would come to such a small village in this remote area of the country, so he felt confident that he would find none there.

Nearing a small house on the outskirts of the remote village, he saw an old man working in the garden next to the house. The preacher approached him and told him that he was a minister preaching the Word of God.

Upon hearing the phrase, "preaching the Word of God," the man stopped his work and invited him into his house. He offered him some hot tea, bread, and cheese. The preacher prayed with the man before eating his food and thanked the man for sharing his food. After eating and thanking the man once again, the preacher asked him if he knew of a larger village nearby with more believers.

The man replied, "Yes. Follow that road over there, and you will arrive by nightfall. Be very careful. The communists were here two weeks ago looking for a minister!"

Graciously thanking the man for his hospitality, he walked down the road toward the larger village. He reflected on how the bread, cheese, and hot tea had certainly been a treat after hiding and surviving on berries for twenty to twenty-five days in the forest. As he continued walking on the road toward the next village, his mind thought back to how he had miraculously escaped from the two, armed guards. However, he was very sad that the communists had killed Mr. Kazakoff.

Now, he alone must carry the burden of the cross. He would continue to do God's work. Although he was physically alone, God's Spirit was always with him. God would always guide him wherever he went. As it is stated, "The Lord is my light and my salvation; whom should I fear? The Lord is the strength of my life; of whom should I be afraid?" (Ps. 27:1).

As the sun set and darkness slowly settled over the forest, the preacher looked around and realized that it would be wise for him to pick up the pace if he wanted to reach the village before it became completely dark. Before long, he rounded a bend in the road and saw lights up ahead. As he approached the village, he stopped and listened to singing, which came from one of the buildings. It was the same kind of music he had heard when he had run away from the monastery.

Momentarily, he thought about why he and his brother had run away from the monastery and how frightened he had been. He had been so fearful that somebody might recognize him as a runaway and might take him back to the monastery, he had quickly backed up into the shadows and had stayed hidden. After the people had left the area and it had become quiet, he had quickly gotten up and had disappeared into the night.

Now, he didn't have to disappear. He was not a runaway. He wanted to go in, to listen to the beautiful music, and to share the gospel with them. He wanted to burst into the building and tell them the plan of salvation.

Suddenly, fear clutched his heart once again as he remembered the fate of Mr. Kazakoff. He had to be extra careful going into the building. He had no way of knowing if communists were in this church or in this village?

Fear of the communists gripped his entire body. He decided to say nothing. They had just killed Mr. Kazakoff, therefore, it was dangerous for him there. They might recognize him and arrest him right there in the church. He knew that they were looking for him everywhere.

The preacher quietly went in, sat down, listened to the message, and said nothing. After the service, one of the church members approached him and asked who he was and where he was going. Father replied that he was a stranger passing through town, who had heard the singing and had wanted to come in and listen to the beautiful music.

For some reason, he began to relax. He did not fear the people here as he had done in some of the other villages where he had stopped and had visited. Rather, he felt as if he was among friends in this village.

He thanked the people for allowing him to be part of the worship service and to listen to the beautiful music. With those words, the preacher turned around and walked out the door.

One of the church members followed him and asked, "Brother, do you have a place to stay for the night?"

Father answered, "No."

"We would love for you to come spend the night in our home, and then in the morning, you can continue on your journey."

Father said, "Yes. I would like that very much."

Because he was still very fearful and cautious, he was afraid to discuss the incident that had taken place about four weeks ago. He did not know whom he could and could not trust. Therefore, he decided that he would say very little. He would just thank the people for the food they provided, for accepting him into their homes, and for sheltering him from the night.

The preacher had a restful night. He got up and prayed the next morning before the sun rose and then traveled to the next village. Again, he thanked the couple for sheltering him from the night and for providing food for him. He also prayed with them and then began walking.

The man had told father to go east on the road. After walking one day, he would come to a fork in the road. He must remember that the well-traveled, wide road that had many people walking, riding horses, and driving wagons went straight south to a large community called Omsk. He told him not to go there, because that was a communist-controlled settlement. He was to take the narrow path that went east away from the communist-controlled area. There he would come across many small villages that would receive him with open arms and would want him to share the Bible with them.

As he walked, he noticed that the villages were getting larger and had more people in them. He thought that was good, and yet, it could be bad too. He passed through a small bazaar (farmers' market) in one of the villages. He went to the bazaar, mingled with the people there, and looked over all the fruits and fresh vegetables that they had displayed for sale.

Many people milled around the fruit and vegetable stands. He overheard some people mention a church service that was happening that night. As he continued to listen, he learned that an evangelical group was meeting. Excitedly, he struck up a conversation with one of these men and asked the time and the place of the meeting. He also asked if strangers were welcome.

The man said, "Yes. Of course! This is an open meeting. Everybody is invited." He added, "Jesus did not invite only the Jews. He went out and ministered to everybody."

The preacher was very glad that he had talked to the gentleman. He told himself that he would go and listen to the sermon. He thought, *I wonder if they are going to have beautiful singing in the service?*

The preacher ended up staying in the village for about a week. He became well acquainted with most of the people in the church. He finally told them that he was a young minister who loved to preach the Bible.

An elderly couple approached him after the service and invited him to stay with them and discuss the Bible as long as he was in that village. They wanted to learn more about the Bible.

The preacher stayed in the village for about a week or so.

Father felt very comfortable with the people in this village. They all were eager to learn more about the Bible. During his stay in the village, he visited many homes, praying and discussing the Bible with the people there.

Chapter 8

New Perspectives in God's Ministry

The following Sunday after the morning church service, two deacons from the little church approached and questioned the preacher about his faith. Apparently satisfied by his answers, they agreed to let him preach that night.

After the evening service, one of the deacons came to him and said, "There are not too many young men like you who are dedicated to preaching the gospel. You need to study and to learn more about the Bible so you can be a stronger witness for our Lord Jesus Christ. **You may be one of the chosen ones selected by God to spread his Word to other nations!**

"You need to go to the First Evangelical Baptist Convention in Siberia next month. Ministers will be there who would love to hear you and teach you to become a stronger witness. They want to help you understand the Bible more and will also teach you how to reach more people for Christ."

That sounded very exciting to the preacher. He said, "Yes. I want to go there. I want to learn more about the Bible."

The deacon continued, "Ministers will be there who have studied the Bible all of their lives. Others have preached the Bible their whole lives. There will be those who were imprisoned for preaching the gospel and those who have lost their loved ones in prison for preaching the gospel. All those people will gather there because they were united through the blood of our Lord Jesus Christ, who died on the cross, and on the third day arose. It is through His death and resurrection that we have eternal life! We will take up an offering to help you with the expenses to go to the meeting."

Father, overwhelmed with joy, thought, *If Mr. Kazakoff would not have died at the hands of the communists, he would be standing next to me, and we would be planning this trip to the meeting together.*

Chapter 9

Ordination and the First Siberian Evangelical Baptist Convention

(March 14, 1927)

My father was ordained as a Baptist minister in 1926. After his ordination, the First Siberian Evangelical Baptist Convention appointed him as the evangelist for the Siberian Evangelical Baptist Association. In 1927, he went to the very first Evangelical Baptist Convention of Siberia as a delegate representing the Siberian Evangelical Baptist Association.

The First Evangelical Baptist Convention of Siberia met in the capital city of Siberia, called New Siberia. See the photo of the nine ministers who were ordained in Siberia in 1926 and were present at the First Evangelical Baptist Convention of Siberia. All the deacons who were ordained that year in the association were photographed at the convention on March 14, 1927. My father is one of the nine ministers in the photo.

Первое заседание Совета Сибирского Союза Баптистов в гор. Ново-Сибирске 14 марта 1927 г.

Стоят слева направо: И. А. Евстратенко, И. Е. Кондратьев, П. Г. Шилохвостов, Е. С. Белозуб. Сидят слева направо: Ф. И. Кикоть, Ф. М. Папковский, А. С. Ананьин, И. П. Бондаренко, А. А. Кондрашев.

Вести из Сибири.

С 14 по 16-ое марта 1927 г. в Сибирской столице — в г. Ново-Сибирске собралась первая сессия Совета Союза Сибирского братства. Интересно было видеть, как послушно слетелись они — испытанные строители Царства Господня, герои Божьего дела и, при очевидном благословении, разрешали вопросы, связанные с благоустройством наших Сибирских организаций.

Вечерами, в переполненном до отказу помещении местной общины, происходили евангелизационные собрания. Господь мощно влиял на сердца грешников и ежедневно многие души делались достоянием Голгофы. Эти дни были днями духовного подъема. Ново-Сибирск переживал слезы умиления, раскаяния и благодарности к Господу...

К глубокому сожалению нужно отметить тот печальный факт, что в городе нет соответствующего центру молитвенного дома. Полуподвальное помещение, в котором происходят собрания, не может отвечать духовным потребностям нашего дела. Сотни страждущих душ остаются за его дверями. Совет Союза вполне учел это и вынес постановление с настоящего строительного сезона приступить к постройке Союзного молитвенного дома в Ново-Сибирске.

На этом же заседании решено возбудить ходатайство пред Главлитом об издании ежемесячного органа печати ССБ журнала «Свет Истины».

Господь в помощь нашим работникам!

И. Филадельфийский.

3. Photo of the ministers who were ordained in Siberia in 1926 and were present at the Siberian Convention in 1927

Before the ordination service, each new minister was intensely questioned about his belief in the Bible and about Jesus being his personal savior. The questioning of each candidate to be ordained was usually done one or two days before the ordination service. The discussion with each candidate took as long as was necessary to clear up all the issues that were in question and to assure that each candidate was willing to pick up his cross and follow in the footsteps of Jesus for the rest of his life, which might mean persecution, prison, torture, and even death.

All the candidates were repeatedly reminded that many of their brothers and sisters, who had stood their ground and had remained faithful, were being tortured and executed for their beliefs and their stands against communism. For some of them, this ordination might mean they would only serve the Lord in this world for a very short amount of time, but they would gain eternal life with our Lord Jesus Christ!

Keep in mind that Stalinism was at its height during that era. At this time in Russia, communism was thought of as the supreme god of the universe and the future of all people, and the goal was utopia for all. To the communists, religion was considered as opium or poison for the minds of the people. It was a roadblock for communism. Therefore, it had to be eliminated. The ministers who preached about God, Jesus, salvation, and religion were considered heretics and enemies of the state and had to be eliminated, for they poisoned the minds of the masses. Communism was the true god and should be worshiped as such.

Therefore, all the candidates for ordination understood the difficulties they would face by accepting Christ as their personal Savior and for being ordained as ministers. Their lives would be changed forever. All of the newly ordained ministers would be persecuted, imprisoned, tortured, and even killed for their beliefs in Jesus Christ. The Bible says, "Blessed is the man that endures temptation: for when he is tried, he shall receive the crown of life which God had promised to them that love him" (James 1:12).

The candidates knew the Bible well. They were prepared for their new life in Christ. They were prepared to serve our Lord Jesus Christ.

They knew what it meant to live, to suffer, and to die for Christ. All the newly ordained ministers were on fire for the Lord. They wanted to go out and evangelize the whole world. They all had a deep, strong love for the Word of God and for the preaching of His Gospel. All of these newly ordained ministers needed to be challenged with God's work by receiving a church in which to minister.

4. My father was born in 1897, in the village of Zakavrasheno, and in the Province of Siberia, Russia.

5. Photo of my parents after they were married

My mother's family moved to Bogotol, in the Province of Siberia, Russia. There she accepted Christ as her personal Savior and, in May of 1920, was baptized.

My father met my mother (Miss Luba Babina) in New Siberia (the capital of Siberia). One month after the First Siberian Evangelical Baptist Conference in the capital of Siberia, they were married on April 27, 1927.

Because of my father's strong conviction and love for the Word of God, he was appointed as pastor of a much larger church in Siberia. This new church had no pastor. The one who had been there had mysteriously disappeared. Nobody knew what had happened to him. They had told my father, the new pastor, about the situation before assigning this church to him. The new pastor said, "I understand, and I will try to help as much as I can. My wife, Luba, and I will work with the people to help build a stronger church."

Little did the new pastor realize that the communists were behind the problem in the church. Not long after my father started ministering at the new church, certain people in the church told him that he needed to cooperate with the government in order to keep his position as minister. The government wanted to know what every member did and what every sermon he was going to preach about.

"If you cooperate with us," they told him, "you will remain the minister of this church as long as you wish. You also will be guaranteed full-time secular employment. All we ask you to do is to let us know what is going on in your church and what your members are doing. We will work with you and help you to form your proper sermons so the government will not interfere with your church program. It is a very simple request, and we will help you and you help us."

After discussing the situation with the deacon body in the church, the new pastor said, "No, I will not work with them. I cannot betray my God and my church members by preaching communism as the true religion of the people and portraying communism as the supreme god of the universe."

Chapter 10

Practicing What You Preach

My father's bold stand against the communists would begin the communists' persecution of him for his strong belief in God rather than in the Communist Party. This was the place in the road where my father picked up the burden of the cross and carried it for the rest of his life.

The deacon body and the church praised their minister for standing up and not giving in to the pressure by the communists. They assured him, "We will have a lookout before, during, and after each service for these people, as they start coming to our church. We will immediately warn you and get you away from the building quickly, so when they come looking for you, you will not be here."

Eventually, the communists realized what was going on. They shifted their tactics and became more aggressive, demanding to know where the minister was. It was obvious that he, as bold and assertive as he was for preaching the Word of God, was no match for these godless, communist thugs, who would invade his church whenever they pleased and conduct a false inspection while looking for the minister so they could arrest and persecute him.

Eventually it became too much for the church members and the minister to continue playing this cat and mouse game. The communists became more and more aggressive. It was extremely dangerous for the minister and his wife Luba.

One evening during the church service, the communists suddenly raided the church. Not finding the minister in the building, they were very frustrated and vowed to get him sooner or later. They wanted to imprison him for poisoning the minds of the people and turning them against the government.

That evening after the communists left the church building, the deacons had a brief meeting. The subject of the meeting was the minister. Since he refused to cooperate with the communists, the deacon body thought it would be best if he and his wife go somewhere else and work in another church. If not, next time the communists came, they might close the church building and put many of the church members in prison for helping their minister and his wife.

Chapter 11

Cooperate and Live

The deacons informed my father, their minister, of their decision. Their minister reiterated that he had taken an oath to preach the gospel as it was written in Acts 1:8.

He reminded them, "God sacrificed His Son. Through His Son's death and resurrection, He gave me eternal life (John 3:16). Therefore, I can do nothing else but preach the Word of God like Jesus commanded me to do."

Some members of the congregation said, "For your own safety and the safety of the church, cooperate with them just a little bit. Just long enough for us to grow and be much stronger. Then we will go against them full force and will continue to grow. God will take care of the communists."

However, the minister said, "No. We must proclaim the Word of God as He commanded us to do!" The deacons replied that if he didn't cooperate with them, the communists would kill him. He would disappear at night, and nobody would know what had happened to him, just like the last minister who was there. He had also been on fire for the Lord. He had refused to talk to anybody or cooperate with them.

"One night, The head Deacon stated that their last Minister and his family disappeared, and to this day, nobody knows what happened to him or his family. We don't want that to happen to you. Please cooperate just a little bit to show them that you are working with them. You don't have to do everything they say. Just pretend that you're working with them. Agree with them outwardly, but within your heart, you continue to serve the Lord in the church as a true servant of God. The church will know that you are a true servant of God."

The minister said, "No. I cannot. I cannot betray my Lord Jesus Christ, who died for me and gave me eternal life. I also cannot betray Mr. Kazakoff, my brother in Christ, recently killed by the communists for preaching the Word of God. I was ordained to proclaim the Gospel to the world, and that is what I intend to do. God's Word cannot be compromised. Jesus did not try to compromise or bargain with God. He voluntarily died on the cross. Through His death and resurrection, He gave us eternal life (John 3:16). He ordered us to proclaim his gospel around the world (Acts 1:8). That is what I intend to do—carry out His commission."

Needless to say, the church asked the minister to leave before the communists came back and closed the church down completely.

They said, "When they come looking for you, we will tell them that you left and did not leave a forwarding address."

The minister said that he understood their situation. He thanked them for giving him the opportunity to share the Gospel with them.

That night after the communists left, the minister and his wife quickly got their things together and left without telling anybody where they were going. They knew that their lives were in danger and that they must get away from there as quickly as possible.

Before they left the church that night, some of the deacons told the minister that it would be safer for him to go and preach in smaller villages where there was no communist control yet. As they were getting ready to walk away from the house where they staying, one of the devout deacons approached and told them to stay away from big towns. The communists were in the big towns but had not infiltrated the small villages yet.

"Go and preach in the small villages. God will bless you as you proclaim the gospel to all people."

The minister and his wife walked out of the yard and headed toward the road.

The deacon asked them, "Where are you going? So we will know."

The minister said, "We don't know. But God knows. He will guide us where He wants us to go and serve Him."

The minister and his wife spread the Gospel by holding services in small churches and teaching others about the Word of God. They avoided the communists at all costs. They continued their ministry as they walked from one small village to the next across the southern province of Siberia.

Chapter 12

Fleeing South toward China

They made their way south across the cold Siberian countryside and into southern Russia as they headed in the direction of China. My father heard that China was a free country. It was a good place to proclaim the Gospel, live, and raise a family.

While fleeing southward, he remembered what the deacon had told him: Stay away from big towns. Preach the Word of God in small villages and towns where there are no communists. That way they would be free to travel and to preach the Word of God. He remembered and continued to do exactly what he had been told.

He and Luba started a family. The first addition to their family was Tava. Tava was born September 17, 1929, in Zakavrasheno, Siberia. Then a year later, Tony came on the scene. Tony was born in Djarkent, Russia, on June 1, 1930. The third addition to the family while on their journey from Russia to China was little Vera.

As they continued going south from one village to another, all the people welcomed them with open arms. These people were hungry for the Word of God. They listened intently as my father preached the Gospel to them. After the service, they asked many questions about the Bible, which my father answered.

The church members of one small village told my father that this was the last village before reaching the Chinese border, which was about two hundred and fifty miles away.

He said, "From here you must travel at night and hide during the day. The communists will be watching this road very closely. If they catch you, they will send you back to Siberian labor camps. There will be no more villages between here and China. It may take you eighteen to twenty days to reach the Russian Chinese border from here. You must be very careful. The communists are everywhere between here and the border. They will do their best to try to catch you before you reach the Chinese border."

Thus far, the church members had been very gracious, providing transportation from one village to another. With three young children, the little family, now more than ever, needed transportation to reach China. Father did not have any money and therefore could not afford to buy a horse.

After the service, one of the church members approached Father and said, "You need a big strong horse for your wife and your children. I have a big horse that I will give you. He is too old to pull heavy logs in the field like he used to do, but he still has a lot of life left in him. He is a big horse and very strong. Your wife and your children can easily ride him all the time. I cannot use him here on the farm, but he will be a big help to you and your family. We did not know what we were going to do with him. We were going to sell him. But we felt very uncomfortable about selling this big, beautiful horse. We prayed about it, and God laid it on our heart to give this horse to you for God's glory."

The farmer gave father two large sacks. "I will sew them together for you. They will be like homemade saddlebags, except instead of leather, they are made out of sackcloth. They will not tear. They are very strong and will easily support the children. Place them over the horse's back behind where your wife sits. Place one child in each sack on the horse's back, with your wife sitting in front of the sacks. Or your wife could place the sacks with the children in front of her. That way, she can watch them more closely. She will have to hold the third, the youngest one, in her arms.

"You, dear brother, will lead the horse. You do not have to buy any food for the horse this time of year. There's plenty of grass everywhere. There's also plenty of water everywhere. You see how God provided for your need and made us feel good about giving the horse to you for God's glory instead of selling the horse?"

When they had traveled south toward the Chinese border for several days, Father noticed that the vegetation was getting very scarce and water was very hard to find. They walked at night and hid during the day. After traveling about ten nights, they ran out of food and water.

Father took the family to a small low area, away from the road, and behind some large rocks. He told Mother to stay hidden behind the rocks with the children.

He said, "Make sure that they stay quiet so nobody will know you're hiding behind the rocks. And I will take the horse and go look for water and food."

Father left before dawn. All day long, the family kept peeking around the big rocks looking for father. They didn't see him. The day turned into a cold night, and Mother huddled behind the rocks with her three children and tried to stay warm. Now they were very frightened. Father had not come back!

They cried from hunger and the cold, but Mother hushed them. "Quiet! Don't cry. We don't want the bad people to find us and hurt us."

Mother spent most of the night talking softly to the three children in order to keep them from crying. Early the next morning, Mother spotted Father walking toward them, leading the horse. Father had found food and water for the horse and his family.

The children immediately wanted the water and the food. Father carefully rationed out the water and the food. He gave one ration to each of them. It reminded them of when a mother bird feeds her baby birds. They hungrily reach out toward her mouth for the food.

After Father gave some food to the three children, he gave a small portion to his wife. Then he finally took a small portion for himself. He and Mother prayed and thanked God for a safe return and for the food and water that he was able to get for the family and the horse. They stayed hidden behind the big rocks, rested all day, and waited for darkness before leaving.

They continued to walk south toward the Russian border for many nights. During the second week of walking, Father spotted headlights in the distance coming toward them from the opposite direction. This meant that they were getting close to the Russian Chinese border.

Immediately after spotting the headlights, Father guided the horse and his family off the road. He wanted them to be as far away from the road as possible so they would not be seen. He did not want to take any chances. He did not want the people in the rapidly approaching vehicle to see them.

As the headlights came closer to the area where the family was, Father saw two trucks on the road, which were probably loaded with Russian communist soldiers heading away from the Russian Chinese border. The soldiers were being transported back to their home base after working their shift on the border.

Now Father knew that they were getting close to the Chinese border. There were always more soldiers at the border. Father and the family were very careful and always on the alert. They did not want to be caught this close to the border. The communists would surely kill them or send them to labor camps in Siberia.

A member of one of the churches had given Father and Mother an old, broken sewing machine.

He had said, "Here. Take this. If you can fix it, it's yours."

Father had eagerly taken the sewing machine, had looked at it, and had said that yes, he thought he could fix it and make it work. They had taken the sewing machine with them on their journey south.

Here at the border, Father knew that if they were caught with the sewing machine, they would be accused of transporting contraband. The soldiers would confiscate it immediately and arrest them. The soldiers would take them to prison and send Father to the Siberian labor camps to work and eventually to be executed.

Father decided to bury the sewing machine in the sand by a tree. He marked the tree and the spot so he would know where to look for it later. He planned to come back when it was safe. He would dig it up, take it home, fix it, and use it. Six months later, Father went back to the border and found the old sewing machine, brought it back, fixed it, and Mother used it for a long time to make and mend clothes.

Chapter 13

Night River Crossing into China

Father and mother walked next to the horse each night. They took turns carrying Tava in their arms. The two younger children were in the homemade, cloth saddlebags on the horse's back. They were very peaceful because the rocking motion created by the horse relaxed them, thus lulling them to sleep. Resting and hiding during the day, the family walked under the cover of darkness at night.

After walking about twenty nights, Father said, "I think we're very close to the border. I hear water rushing over rocks. We must be very close to the river that separates Russia and China." They walked toward the sound of the water.

They feared the communists. The communists patrolled both sides of the river at the border. My parents knew that they were there. They didn't know how far away they were. Father prayed that the communists would be a long way from them and would not hear them crossing the river.

As they approached the riverbank, they heard the sound of rushing waters and rapids much more clearly than before. They stood there and listened to the deafening sound of the rushing water.

Father said to Mother, "You stay here with the horse and the babies. I will go along the river bank and find the safest place for us to cross the river." He returned shortly and said, "This is a very good place for us to cross. The river is wider and shallower here than other places."

As the family neared the water, Father stopped and said, "Let us pray." He thanked God for the safety of the trip thus far, for the food, and for all the people that had helped them. Then he prayed for God's will regarding their trip to China and proclaiming the gospel there. He prayed, "Please help us to cross this river safely and continue to guide us where You want us to go."

As he stood there in the darkness by the river, Father thought about the best and safest way to cross the border into China without being spotted by the communist guards. He could ride a horse across the river while carrying one child at a time into China, take his wife across the river first and then bring the infants, which would mean greater risk and exposure to the communists, or make one trip. He chose one trip.

He put the children in the makeshift saddlebags and his wife on the horse. He would lead the horse across the river. Two children would be in the saddlebags placed in front of Mother. Mother would hold the third child tightly with her left hand and the horse's mane with her right. There was greater risk of an accident and all of them drowning in the river this way, but there was a fighting chance that they would survive, if God was willing.

Their best chance for survival was trying, at all costs, to cross the river into China immediately! If they turned around and went back to Russia now, it would mean certain death for Father and the family. Worst of all, they would force him to watch the execution of his family and then would send him to a labor camp in Siberia. That, in itself, would be certain death for him. Therefore, that was not an option.

They must cross the river into China as quickly as they could and while it was still dark. They had to hurry before the communist guards patrolling the border discovered them. Once they crossed into China, they would be safe. As he and his wife stood next to the horse at the water's edge, he momentarily froze and broke out in a cold sweat. He pictured his family crossing this perilous river in darkness. Crossing this raging river with its strong currents and undertows was very dangerous. He pictured them being swept down river by the strong current and drowning.

Suddenly, something jarred him. He realized that they could not hesitate there any longer. They must cross the river immediately and without hesitation. This decision would mean life or death. Those two words kept spinning in his mind. *Life or death?* Which was it going to be? If they hesitated much longer, they would die. The border guards would soon be passing by and would catch and kill them. Father thought, *If we cross now without hesitation, we will live—if God is willing.*

He looked at his wife standing next to him and said, "Let's put you on the horse with the babies in front of you—one baby in each sack on either side of the horse. With your right hand, you will hold on very tightly to the horse's mane, and with your left hand, you will hold Tava tightly against your chest."

Luba pleaded, "No, no. I can't do it! I can't swim. I can't swim. I'll fall off the horse and drown. I will drop the baby and she will drown. I can't do this. Let's go back. It is much safer back there."

Father tried to help her up on the horse against her will. She resisted, frantically grasped him with a deadly grip, and refused to let go of him. She refused to get on the horse. She was certain that she was going to die. He finally calmed her down and boosted her onto the horse.

He placed her right hand on the horse's mane and said, "Here. Hold on tight. Now take and hold little Vera with your left hand." She continued to mumble that it was too dangerous and she couldn't do it. She insisted that she was going to drown and that it was too dangerous. They couldn't do this. They would all drown in the river.

Father looked up at her as she sat on the horse, clutched its mane, and held Vera tightly to her chest.

With his usual soft, soothing voice, Father said, "You will be okay. Just hold onto the horse and the baby, and we will make it."

Slowly he led the horse into the river. About halfway across, it got much deeper. The current was much stronger, and it rushed and swirled against and around Father, almost causing him to lose his grip on the horse's bridle and pulling him down stream to his death. Struggling simultaneously to keep his footing on the river bottom and to lead the horse proved to be too much! The strong current almost swept him off his feet!

The only thing Father could do was reach the horse's mane and hold on. He quickly moved to the side of the horse, grabbed the horse's mane, and walked next to the horse instead of in front of it. The large horse shielded Father from the strong, raging water. The powerful current did not seem to bother the horse at all. The horse walked across the river with ease. Many times, Father felt he had lost his footing, but the horse kept dragging him along.

The horse kept slowly moving forward. It was as if he knew and sensed the danger surrounding them and that their safety depended on his strength. Finally, Father realized that he could touch the bottom again—his feet were on the ground. He walked next to the horse. The water was not as swift or as deep as they approached China's side of the river. Father still clung to the horse's mane as he struggled to keep up with its pace.

At last, the horse pulled them onto dry ground on China's side of the river. There the horse stopped. It was as if he knew that everybody was safe and needed to rest. Father, holding his wife's hand, realized that they were all safe. He prayed aloud, thanking God for keeping them safe as they crossed the river into China and for the big, strong horse that was given to them.

They rested there for a moment and then started walking away from the riverbank toward the road. Father knew that the communists always patrolled both sides of the river. Therefore, they were not out of danger yet. That night the moon was shining brightly, and they were able to walk a good distance from the river into a clump of trees where they bedded down for the rest of the night to dry off and rest before going on.

Just before dawn, Father was awakened by voices in the distance. He raised his head and listened intensely. Yes, it was men's voices speaking Russian. The men must have been in a very jovial mood because they were laughing, singing, and joking. They were communist soldiers going back to Russia after patrolling China's side of the river. Father immediately ducked back into the bushes and made sure that the family stayed quiet until the communist soldiers had passed that area.

By the time the soldiers were gone, it was early dawn. Father quietly got the family up and put the saddlebags on the horse's back. Then

Father and Mother placed one child in each sack. On this day, Mother decided to walk with Father. They took turns carrying Tava. She was feisty and energetic and wanted to walk next to Mother. Of course, she was just too small and could not keep up with the pace of her parents, who were walking next to the horse. Even though they walked very slowly, she could not keep up. She would tire out very quickly and have to be picked up and carried by one parent or the other.

Walking during the day was much easier. They tried to stay off the main road as much as possible. After walking for half a day, they saw, some distance away from the road, a house with what appeared to be a flour mill. Father hoped that he would be able to work at the flour mill in exchange for food and a place for the family to stay, so they headed for the house in front of the flour mill.

Chapter 14

The Road to Kuldja

As they approached the gate to the front yard, a man walked very quickly out of the house, across the yard, and out the gate. He then made sure that the gate closed behind him, thus signaling by his actions to Father and Mother that he did not want them close to his house.

He approached my father and asked, "Are you lost? Do you need directions to go to Russia?"

Father explained to the man that he was a Baptist minister on his way to China to do God's work. He asked the man if he would allow Father to work in the mill while the family rested for a few days.

The man said, "No. The communists are everywhere. They're looking for Russian people without documents to take back to Russia. You look like a white Russian. They will come here, catch you and your family, and punish us for hiding you. So please go away. We don't want to get into trouble with the communists.

"Here. Take these two big loaves of bread and this sack of corn for the horse. You will need this food for you and your horse to have enough strength to reach the next village in about four or five days walking. Stay away from the main road; the communists are everywhere."

Curiosity got the best of the man. He asked my father, "Where are you going?"

Father replied, "We want to go to Kuldja."

"Ah, Kuldja! Everybody wants to go to Kuldja. Yes. There are many Russian people in Kuldja. Four more days of walking and you'll be close to Kuldja." The man spoke partly in Russian and partly in Chinese. It was difficult, but Father understood him. He thanked the man for the bread and the corn. With his wife standing at his side holding the infant in her arms and the other two children in the sacks on the horse's back, my father turned around and walked in the direction of Kuldja.

Father was quite depressed as he and his wife walked away from the house. He was so sure that the people in the house would help them and let them rest there for a few days. At least the man was gracious enough to give them bread and corn, which they desperately needed.

Looking at his wife, who walked next to him, he said, "I guess those people feared communism more than they feared God. I understand their situation and thank God for the help that they have given us in spite of their fear of communism."

Chapter 15

Kuldja

After walking and hiding for four more days, they finally reached Kuldja. They ran out of food for themselves and for their horse, so Father sold the horse to buy food for the family in Kuldja. Father kept walking up and down the streets looking for a place to live. They didn't understand a word of Chinese, but thankfully, they met a Russian family that owned a three-room house and were willing to rent one room to my father and his family. With the money from the sale of the horse, Father paid for several months' rent and still had money left over for food.

Disease was widespread. People were dying from smallpox, malaria, and dysentery.

Little Vera was very small and frail due to lack of nourishment and was plagued with infantile diseases. The journey had been too much for her malnourished and sickly body. In 1932, shortly after the family reached Kuldja, little Vera died from malnutrition and dysentery. She had survived the journey through Russia and across the Russian Chinese border, only to succumb to malnourishment and the dreaded dysentery, which was plaguing the whole country at that time.

In those days, that area of the world was one big conflict. It had been for hundreds of years. The battle raged on in the northwestern part of China for freedom and independence. The Japanese came in fighting. The communists came from the north, fighting and stirring up trouble among the people in Kuldja. Then a big power struggle in 1934 emerged between the Chinese and the Dunganese, who were Chinese speaking Muslims.

Many other warlords took advantage of the chaotic situation. They battled to control territories in the vast region of Xinjiang, China. This power struggle became a big war involving many ethnic groups in the entire region.

The communists would come across the border at night to stir up trouble, incite riots, and start fights among the ethnic groups. Then they would go back across the border into Russia and act as if they had nothing to do with it.

They watched the ethnic groups slaughter each other. When the situation was right, the communists came across the border from Russia to supposedly stop the violence and clean up the mess (that they had created) under the pretense that they were coming to rescue the Russian people, who were suffering and being persecuted under the present situation. Seeing an opportunity to advance their cause of communism in this province, they crossed the border from Russia on a nightly basis to stir up trouble among the numerous ethnic groups, further fueling the ethnic violence that was escalating in the region.

They came in and took over the entire northwestern province of Xinjiang. This situation, which began as a small, insignificant, local, ethnic conflict, now escalated to a big war involving the Chinese, Dunganese, Turkish Muslims, Russian Jews, and other ethnic groups. All of these people were fighting each other for no reason at all. The communists were the people who had incited this situation and had provoked the people to fight among themselves. Bloodshed was widespread.

The Chinese enlisted all the adult men to fight. Father had just received his Chinese documents. Therefore, he was automatically recruited to fight in this war, which started in early summer and lasted until the spring of 1935. During this time, everybody feared for their lives and stayed inside behind locked doors. Mother and the two children stayed in the room all the time because they were afraid to go out. People were being shot and killed everywhere. The children would sneak out to get firewood and to bring in a bucket of snow to melt on the stove for water.

While my father was at war, my mother and the two children basically survived on bread and water. They had flour that Father had purchased. Mother would bake loaves of bread but would always cut off the ends, dry them, and save them for an emergency. She did not allow the children to eat the dried bread no matter how hungry they were. She kept telling them this was for an emergency. If something happened, they would have this dry bread to eat and to survive on.

They were overjoyed when Father returned from the war in the spring. For his service in the war, he, along with all the other soldiers who served, was given a horse as payment and gratitude for helping the Chinese government.

Although the war was over, living in Kuldja was still very dangerous. My father decided that they should leave and find a safer place to raise a family and minister for God. Father and Mother packed their few belongings and placed them on the horse's back. Then they placed their two children on top of their belongings and set out for a safer place to live.

Because it was early spring, it was cold. The ground was frozen and snow-covered. As they left the town, the sides of the road were littered with bodies, which were half-buried in the snow. Father led mother and the horse through this area and cautioned us, saying, "Be careful, don't step on the bodies; walk around them." They continued as quickly as they could to get away from this area, which resembled a battlefield with bodies everywhere. Father was very fearful and quite concerned for the safety of his wife and children.

After walking for three days, they saw a small village. Just before reaching the village, they saw a big flour mill beside a large house. As they approached the flour mill, they noticed that other people, who had fled from the war-torn province, had arrived and were living there. The owners allowed Father, Mother, and the two children to live there also. Father worked at the mill to help pay for their food and their room.

After working and living at the mill for six to seven months and hearing that everything was quiet and back to normal in Kuldja,

Father again loaded the horse with their few belongings, placed the two children on their horse, and with his wife at his side, they started walking back to Kuldja.

When they arrived in Kuldja, they had very little food left and no place to stay. He asked a farmer in the area if they could stay in his barn for several days until they found a room in town. The farmer agreed to that.

Father walked all over town looking for an apartment or room to rent but was unsuccessful. On the third day, he found something. A family of three, a mother, daughter, and older son lived together. They had a nice house with a large yard. There was a well in the middle of the yard. There was a small house in the backyard. The mother was ill and agreed to let them live in the small house if Mother would bake bread, cook, and clean for them. Father, Mother, and the two children moved into the small house in the back.

Mother cooked, cleaned, and helped the people that had given them a place to stay. By this time, my parents had added a boy named Ben and a girl named Lydia to their family. Now there were four children. Tava, being the oldest, was responsible for taking care of the three younger children.

Many times, Mother had to work outside the home after she finished cooking, baking, and cleaning for the lady. She did this to help support the family. She would come home at lunch to feed the children before going back to work for somebody else. Her children were so happy to see her they didn't even care if they ate. They just wanted to be with her. They wanted her to hold them and take care of them. They didn't want her to leave but knew she had to go to work to bring home food for the family.

Father continued to look for steady work. He was always questioned about his belief in communism. He knew that God would eventually guide him to the right place for work. One day, a neighbor told him that he could go and pan for gold in a mountain stream about ten miles from town.

So Father and Tony rode out there on the horse, found the stream, and started panning for gold. By evening, two men showed up and told

Father that he was on government property and could not pan for gold there. If he didn't leave, they would take him and his son and put them in jail. Father recognized these men as communists and knew they had been watching him the entire time he had been in China. So he picked up Tony and the few items he had with him and went back to town.

The family was very happy while they lived in the small house. The woman's son, their landlord, was a very nice man, who was highly educated. They treated the family well, and Mother worked hard while caring for their ill mother. After they had lived in the small house for about two years, the woman passed away and Mother's services were no longer needed. Therefore, they had to move again and find a new place to live.

Chapter 16

Tekes

6. Photo of Alex 3 years old and George 5 years
old, in Kuldja. My father took and developed this
picture—one of the many skills he acquired.

Once again, there was turmoil in Kuldja and the entire region of Xinjiang. Skirmishes between the Chinese, Japanese, Muslims, and Dunganese were heating up. The communists were again taking advantage of all this turmoil and slowly advancing from Russia into the area.

Father wanted to move quickly before he and his family were caught in the middle of the war. He asked a neighbor, who had a big wagon, if he would take them to Tekes, a town located about fifty miles south of there. So the next morning, the neighbor brought his wagon and horses and helped father and the older boys load the wagon with all of the family's belongings.

When they arrived in the town of Tekes, they realized that it was almost a desert—that part of the country had few trees and very little vegetation of any kind. After living there a short time, they realized that fuel was very precious.

Part of the children's responsibility was to gather fresh manure when the nomadic people drove their herds through the village into the mountains. Mother would get them up before dawn and give each one of them a bucket. As the herds came through, everybody in the neighborhood rushed behind the herd and frantically collected fresh, soft manure to fill their buckets. They would hurriedly run home, empty their buckets, and then run back for more. This was one of the few free sources of fuel, which was available in that part of the country. After they collected all the manure, they would bring it home, make it into cakes, dry the cakes, and stack them to use as fuel.

When Father heard that things had calmed down and had returned to normal in Kuldja, he asked a friend to take them back there. The man asked, "Why do you want to go back there? It is much safer here." Father answered that there were many Russian people in that town, and they needed him to preach the gospel to them.

Chapter 17

Moving Back to Kuldja

The next day, Father's friend came with a big wagon pulled by two horses. They loaded the family and their belongings onto the wagon. Tony rode in a small two-wheeled cart pulled by a small pony. My father loaded the cart with caged chickens and their feed.

On the second day, my father realized that Tony was no longer behind us. They stopped the wagon. Father unhitched one of the horses from the wagon, rode back, and looked for Tony and his two-wheeled cart and pony. He rode quite a ways back, asking everyone he passed if they had seen Tony on the road somewhere, but the answer was always the same—no.

Father finally found the little cart and the pony at an inn where Tony had stopped to rest for the night. He was only twelve years old and was doing a man's work. He was exhausted, cold, hungry, and very scared. His pony wasn't able to keep up with the big horses, which were pulling the wagon.

As he got farther and farther behind, he could no longer see the family wagon. It was getting cold and dark. When he saw the inn, he stopped there to rest. He went inside and asked the owner if he could sleep in the barn, which had a wood-burning stove already lit. Since Tony had no money, he gave the owner some chickens so he could spend the night there. The man agreed and allowed Tony to stay in the barn in exchange for the chickens.

Father was relieved that he had finally found Tony. After spending the night at the inn, Father and Tony joined the rest of the family down the road. They all prayed and thanked God that Father had found Tony and that they were all together again. Then they continued the journey back to Kuldja.

Many more Russian families had moved to the town. They had also fled from communism in Russia. Father looked for a place to stay. He was able to find one, but the landlord, who was a devout Muslim, was very reluctant to allow another Russian family to live in the house. The last Russian family that had lived there had drunk and fought all the time. They had seldom paid their bill, and subsequently, he had had to evict them. Needless to say, his past experience with Russians had not been very good. My father finally convinced the owner that they were a good Christian family that did not drink or smoke and that the owner would have no problems with them.

It was the Muslim custom in that area that after sundown nothing was to be given out to anybody. One day when the fire went out in the house, Mother sent Tava to the landlord's house to get some hot coals to start our fire. She went in and asked the landlady for coals. The landlady said, "No. It is too late. You come back tomorrow, and I will give you fire. It is too late today. You come tomorrow before the sun goes down. Then I will give you fire."

When the landlord heard about this, he told his wife, "They must have fire tonight. Give it to them in spite of what the Muslim law says. They are good people with many children in the family. They must have the fire tonight!" So Tava got the coals to start the fire that night. They lived there for five or six years. Life there was good. The landlord was very happy with them and told father that they could live there as long as they liked.

One day while Mother, Tava, and Tony were working in the potato field chopping weeds, a wagon pulled up with a man and two women in it. The man got out of the wagon and approached Mother in the field. After greeting them, the man proceeded to tell Mother that they were going to Tekes, which was about fifty miles away. He said that their *babuska* (grandmother) was too old and would never survive the trip. He asked, "Would you be kind enough to allow her to stay with you until we get back? She is a good, hardworking woman and will not cause you any trouble. Take good care of our grandmother until we get back. We will come back in two weeks to pick her up and take her home with us.

Mother said that it would be okay. She could stay with the family until the man came back to pick her up. The elderly lady immediately crawled out of the back of the wagon, marched straight into the field, greeted everybody with a big smile, and said that her name was Anna. Although she looked as old as the hills, she was bright-eyed, bushy-tailed, and full of energy. She did not waste any time. She grabbed a hoe and started chopping weeds along with the rest of us.

The man and the woman got back into their wagon, waved, and said goodbye as they happily prepared to ride on to their destination without the excess baggage—their babushka. Apparently, their babushka would have prevented them from having a carefree vacation or visit with friends of their own age. She would not have fit into their group, which would have caused them embarrassment. They would not have known what to do with her. Now the problem was solved, and she would not be a thorn in their side or keep them from having a good time.

The man looked back at them, almost in a hesitant and regretful manner. He was probably thinking they should not have left their grandmother with total strangers. Most likely, mixed emotions flooded his heart with guilt. His thoughts were quickly interrupted by the sudden, jerky, forward movement of the wagon, which required his immediate attention. As the wagon rolled forward on the bumpy, dusty dirt road, the man, once again, turned his head toward them and in a loud voice shouted, "Babushka, we will come back and pick you up in two weeks. We will take you home with us."

However, Babushka acted as if she didn't hear a word he said. The old lady apparently did not care one way or the other. She had had enough of them. She had acted like she wanted to get away from them. Now, she focused on her clothes, which her relatives had thrown on the road as they happily rode off to their destination. Anna quickly picked up her bundle of clothes and placed them in the field where we were working. She then joined us chopping weeds in the potato field.

Anna was very helpful around the house as well. She never wasted time but always found something to do. She washed and cleaned the clothes daily and mended all the children's torn clothes with old rags that she found, cleaned, and used as patches.

Most of the time, the patches did not match the color of the clothes. That did not matter. The patch covered up the hole and repaired the torn shirt or pair of pants. In fact, it made the garments more colorful. The children would argue, saying, "Our patches are more colorful than your patches. Then one of them would run up to Babushka and ask her to put another beautiful patch on his or her pants or shirt.

Sometimes the children would intentionally tear a hole in their clothes just to get more patches. Soon Mother had to step in and stop the game of tearing the clothes to create new holes in the shirts or pants.

Anna helped Mother cook meals for the family. She worked in the garden along with the rest of the family. As time went by, she became part of the family.

She was not a very talkative person and kept to herself. When we asked, "Where do you live?" She would simply respond that she lived over there and not too far from here. She would raise her hand and point in the direction from which she had come.

"In a small village in that direction. Over there," she would say as she pointed again in that direction. "In the village over there, not too far from here."

It was obvious that her world was very small. This was possibly the first time in her life she had been out of her village.

The family found out that Anna could not read or write. When Father or Mother read the Bible in the evening to the family, Anna was always very interested and listened intently. She would always have questions for my father or mother about the Bible and the passages they had read that evening. She was very happy after they finished the Bible reading and closed with a word of prayer.

When the family gathered for a meal, they would begin and end the meal with a prayer. Anna was always the first and the loudest one to say, "Amen," after each prayer.

Two years went by, and Anna was still with them. She became part of the family and was treated as such. They took care of her, and she appreciated it.

Eventually her relatives came back from Tekes, picked her up, and took her home with them. The family never heard from her or her relatives again. To this day, they still don't know who they were, where they were from, or where they lived. This was a classic description of how my parents treated everybody. They shared what they had with others and gave others what they needed, within reason.

7. Photograph of Tava, Anna, Tony and Mother in the potato field

After the family settled in its new place, Father bought a cow. She was a very bad cow. No one could get close enough to her to milk her because she would kick and move around. My father took her back and traded her for another cow. This new cow was very good. She gave them a lot of milk and was good-natured.

It was a good thing too, because Mother had more children. First, she had twins—a boy named George and a girl named Nida. Tava was about nine years old at that time. Father built a large cradle that fit both babies. Everything was good until a smallpox epidemic broke out, and they lost their little girl, Nida, at the age of six months. Vaccinations were not available in those days, especially in that part of the country. Therefore, the smallpox epidemic claimed many lives. There was only one country doctor for the whole territory, and he did not know what to do.

The family faced many hardships, such as death, smallpox, dysentery, starvation, and cold. Other children in their family did not survive due to other challenges at that time. Eighteen children were born to our parents, including three sets of twins. I am the only one of the twins who survived. Eight children survived to embark on the long, incredible journey of faith from Russia to America.

Our mother knitted hats and socks for small children. Because white yarn was cheaper, Mother would buy it and then dye it pretty colors. She would leave home early in the morning, before the men left their houses for work, and go door-to-door selling the knitted items. Kids liked them very much, and fathers would buy them for their children.

By lunchtime, she sold all of her items and came home. She did this to earn extra money to support the family and to buy what she needed to bake bread and sweets for the family during the holidays. On rare occasions, she would buy meat. Meat was very expensive and few people could afford it.

However, they had lots of different fruits and vegetables in the summer. When the fruit was ripe, the family would go to the orchards and pick apricots, apples, and other fruits. They would dry the fruits for the owner. The owner would then pay them for drying the fruit and allow them to take some of the dried fruit home with them. So the family worked the entire season picking and drying fruit. During the summer months, fruits and vegetables were plentiful. The parents were always prepared for winter. They had plenty of dried fruit and canned vegetables.

Prior to Muslim holidays, the Muslim people liked the inside of their homes to be clean and painted. Mother would obtain work from them, painting homes for a couple of weeks. Tava took care of her brothers and sisters while her mother worked. George was about seven months old at that time. At lunchtime, Mother would send someone home with a message that told where she was working that day. Tava, who was waiting outside at noon for the message, would take George to Mother so she could feed him. Then Tava would bring George back to the house.

Father worked as a locksmith and blacksmith in Kuldja, Xinjiang, and Mongolia (See the photocopy of his certificate on next page). When asked where he learned the blacksmith's trade, Father would say he had first been trained on the farm as a teenager and then had worked in a blacksmith's shop in Siberia where he perfected it. Father also learned about electricity when he was a teenager on the farm. He later worked as an electrician in Siberia.

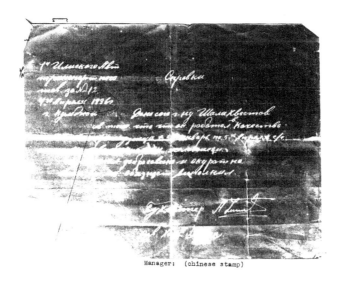

Manager: (chinese stamp)

Mar.26,1951

This is to certify that the above is a true and correct translation
from the Russian language made by the undersigned to her best
knowledge and belief.

Melba Reith

8. Father's Work Certificate and Chinese Stamp

First Iliiskey Auto-
transportation Assoc.
(document)No.12
4th April 1936
KULDJA (Mongolia)

C e r t i f i c a t e :

This is being given to Mr. SHILOHVOSTOFF to
certify that he had worked as a lock-smith -blacksmith
from 5th January to 5th April this year.

He leaves by his own free will. He had worked
consćientiously and diligently and had carried out all
assignments.

signed: A.L . ..signature not clear.
- - - - -
                      bookkeeper
Manager: (chinese stamp)

Mar.26,1951

This is to certify that the above is a true and correct translation
from the Russian language made by the undersigned to her best
knowledge and belief.

NOTARY PUBLIC
In and for the City & County of San Francisco, State of Calif.

MY COMMISSION EXPIRES NOV. 28, 1952
2955 MISSION STREET

9. English translation of certificate

While working as a blacksmith in Kuldja, my father was released from his job because he preached about God and not about communism. His certificate stated that he had resigned or left his position of his own free will.

The certificate was skillfully written and carefully stated that father had not been fired but had voluntarily left the job.

When the communists realize that a person is not in favor of communism but continues to say things against communism and the state, that person is first removed from his or her position. When he or she becomes a threat to the state and communism, that person is discreetly eliminated. That person is said to have left unexpectedly without giving a forwarding address when he or she has actually disappeared during the night and nobody knows what has happened to him or her.

Chapter 18

Almost Frozen to Death

While the family was living in Tugustaral, a small village about thirty miles outside of Kuldja, a man approached my father and mother. He said he would pay Tony and Tava to go into the woods, chop some firewood for his sauna, and bring it to him. Mother thought it was too late in the day and that they should go the next day to get it, but Tony said, "We can do it today. I'll hitch the horse to the sleigh. We will go quickly, chop the firewood, load it on the sleigh, and bring it home before dark."

Mother and Father again said that it was too late in the day. "Let them wait until tomorrow. Tomorrow you will have all day to chop the firewood, bring it over, and give it to the man." However, Tony and Tava were very stubborn. They insisted on going that afternoon. They said they would be back before nightfall, hitched the horse to the sleigh, and rode off into the woods. They quickly chopped the firewood, loaded the sleigh, and were on their way back when a blizzard hit.

It was bitterly cold, very windy, and snowing. Tony and Tava took turns running next to the sleigh to stay warm and to keep from freezing. The blinding, swirling, blowing snow hampered them on their journey home.

As the storm intensified, they became very cold and frightened. They both got on the sleigh. The horse slowly followed the trail that led toward their village and home. Animals have a natural instinct to find their way home. As the horse slowly followed the trail, which was partially covered by drifting and blowing snow, it came to a sudden stop. It was so disoriented, confused, and blinded by the swirling and blowing snow that it just stopped in its tracks.

A local Muslim lady was herding her goats back to her yurt with her dog. She had been caught in the storm as well but had been very close to her yurt. Her dog began to bark fiercely and ran in the wrong direction. She called the dog back, but he did not listen to her voice. As he continued to bark loudly, the lady became curious and followed the dog's barking.

She soon realized that he was barking at a sleigh, which was loaded with firewood and had two children huddled on top of it. Because they were completely covered with snow, they appeared to be frozen. The lady led her goats and their horse and sleigh to her yurt. After taking the children inside her yurt, she went outside and tended to their horse. Then came back into the yurt and covered them with animal hides.

Next, she began to rub their hands and feet, keeping it up most of the night. By early morning, they started to move. She continued to rub their hands and feet more vigorously until they were awake. After covering them up with more goatskins and sheepskins, she kept on rubbing their hands and feet to increase the circulation in their bodies.

Toward midmorning, they started to move, more and more, and opened their eyes. The lady was very happy that they were alive and prepared some hot goat's milk, goat's cheese, and flatbread for them. By late morning, they felt much better. The lady put them back on their sleigh, which was still loaded with firewood and sent them home.

10. Photo of lady cooking in front of her yurt

This is a similar type of dwelling to the one that the Muslim lady lived in. She brought Tava and Tony in from the blizzard and revived them!

Father and Mother did not sleep all night because they were so worried about the two children. The blizzard was fierce with heavy snow swirling and blowing. Throughout the night as they paced the floor, they would periodically open the door and look out through the blinding, driving snow, hoping to see the children nearing the house.

By early dawn, the storm had subsided, and it was a clear morning. By late morning, the parents were very anxious and were ready to leave the house to look for the children. Just about that time, the kids pulled up to the house in the sleigh loaded with firewood. They told their parents what had happened to them after they had cut the firewood and had been on their way home—how they had been caught in a blizzard and had almost frozen to death and about the lady who found them half frozen on the sleigh not too far from her yurt.

Tava and Tony delivered the firewood to the man with the sauna. The children were very happy when the man gave them some money for the firewood. He thanked their parents for allowing the children to get the firewood for him. Father and Mother were very relieved and thanked God that their children were safe. They took the children back to the Muslim lady, thanked her profusely, and gave her half of the money the children had earned for the firewood. They again thanked the lady for finding, saving, graciously feeding, and caring for the children throughout the night.

Chapter 19

The Wall Fell

One day in Tugustaral, a neighbor came over with her son, Sasha, who was our age. She said to him, "Son, why don't you go with George and Alex and take the cow out to the pasture. The three of you can stay out there in the pasture and play."

Shortly after that, Sasha, Alex, and I (George) took the cow out to the pasture to graze. It was quite cold and windy. We huddled together and tried to keep warm in the open field. Then we saw an old adobe wall not far from where we were watching the cow. We decided to go behind the wall to get some protection from the strong, cold wind.

While sitting behind this wall, we dug under the wall and made tunnels through it. Suddenly, somebody screamed, "Run! The wall is falling." I jumped up like a scared rabbit from under the wall. Alex and Sasha sat there laughing. It had been a joke. The wall was not falling.

As it got colder and the wind blew stronger, we got very cold. Alex looked at me and said, "George, go to the house and get us some coats. It is getting very cold out here."

Sasha looked at Alex and said, "Yeah, George, go and get us some jackets. We're very cold." The three of us fussed and argued, and since I was the one who had been appointed first to go after the jackets, I grudgingly crawled from my warm spot behind the wall and headed toward the house.

As I stepped into the house, all the adults were sitting around a samovar (a large Russian teapot) chatting and drinking hot tea. In the lower portion of the samovar, there is a built-in container for hot coals or kerosene, which keeps the water hot. The very top of the samovar is designed to hold a very small teapot, which usually holds the concentrated tea (also kept hot by the coals or kerosene from below)

11. Photo of samovar

They looked at me and asked, "What do you want? You're supposed to be out there watching the cow, not watching us drinking tea in the house!"

"We got very cold, and wanted some jackets to keep us warm while we watch the cow in the pasture," I replied.

Suddenly, the door burst open. Sasha came running into the house crying and screaming, "The wall fell! The wall fell!"

The adults looked at each other, rolled their eyes, shrugged their shoulders, and thought, *No big deal. So the wall fell. What else is new?* At times, strong winds, rain, and other natural elements would erode small sections of an adobe wall, which would eventually fall. It was a common occurrence in that part of the world. Knowing this, the adults continued drinking their hot tea, deeply engaged in their endless, pointless conversation, not giving a second thought to the statement that Sasha had just made!

But Sasha continued to scream in a loud voice, "The wall fell on Alex! He is buried under the wall!" That's when all of the adults dropped what they were doing and ran out of the house as fast as they could, heading toward the pasture. They looked around and saw the cow grazing, but there was no sign of Alex or the wall.

Then Sasha came running up He screamed and pointed to the fallen wall, which was barely visible among the grass and rocks that were everywhere. Sasha led the way to the fallen wall. When they arrived at the wall, they saw nothing but big boulders on the ground where the old adobe wall had been standing. Everybody looked but saw no sign of Alex.

Sasha, still crying, pointed at the center of the fallen wall. The wall, instead of standing upright, had fallen on its side and had broken into large boulders. Most of them were about four feet in diameter and two feet thick. "There, Alex is buried under there!" He pointed to the middle of the fallen wall. "Alex is under there!"

Everybody started looking around the ruins of the adobe wall. They could not see any signs of Alex. Then the neighbor lady, who was walking on top of the boulders, looked down and shouted, "Down there. I see what looks like a shirt under these boulders." As she shouted again, "That must be Alex," she reached down between the boulders and tugged on the shirt. "Yes. It is him!" She continued to tug on the shirt, trying to pull him out.

By now, the rest of the adults had arrived and began to carefully move the big boulders away from his crushed body. They found him buried under the stones, face down. They removed as much dirt from him as possible, carried him away from the fallen wall, and laid him on level ground. After removing more dirt from his face and body, they carefully carried him back to the house. By the time they got Alex into the house and on the bed, he started breathing. Thank God. He was alive!

After making him comfortable on the bed, Father checked him for broken bones. He said that both of his legs were broken in multiple places. His bones were broken above and below the knees. His hips may have been fractured, but there no way to tell. His head and arms seemed to be okay. He breathed heavily but was not complaining of any chest pain.

Father called a Chinese doctor to come and look at Alex and to set the bones in his legs. The next day, the doctor came and set Alex's legs but did not stabilize them with splints.

A week later, Alex still cried and complained of severe pain in his legs. Father noticed that both of his legs were very crooked. Father said, "This is not right. The legs should not be crooked. That's why he's having so much pain." Father called Mother and told her that he must break the legs again, reset them, and put splints on them to make them straight.

Father said to Mother, "You must hold him tight while I rebreak his legs and set them straight. Then I will place splints on either side of his legs. We will bind the splints to his legs so they will not move. That will make the legs heal in the proper position."

When Father started to rebreak Alex's legs, Alex experienced excruciating pain. As father held one of his legs and applied pressure to rebreak it, Alex screamed in agony. As he felt more pressure and the pain intensified, he screamed as loudly as he could—high-pitched, blood-curdling, terrified screams of pain.

Mother instantly let go of Alex's arms and body. She burst into tears and ran out of the room, saying, "I can't do it! I can't hurt my baby. It's too much. I can't handle it. It is too much pain for me and for him to bear. I can't do it!"

Father knew that somebody had to hold Alex so he could work on his legs. He also knew that Mother was too emotional and could not help him. Father went across the street and asked the neighbor lady to help, explaining to her what had to be done. He said, "You must hold him tight and keep him still while I work on his legs. It is going to be very painful for him. He will kick, and he will be screaming, but you must hold him still. If we don't correct his legs now, he may never walk again."

Father repeated everything to her to make sure that she understood what had to be done. Again, he said to her, "Regardless of what happens, don't let him move while I work on his legs. I will tell you when to release him."

She said she understood and was willing to help so that Alex would be able to walk again. Father said that the lady was very calm and eager to help. She held Alex down and kept him from moving while Father rebroke the partially healed bones in his legs. He reset them, put splints on both sides of each leg, and wrapped them firmly. Alex still hurt but no longer screamed in pain.

Toward the end of the day, Alex had settled down and was no longer crying. He only whimpered now and then. He appeared to be more restful and comfortable now than he had been before Father worked on his legs. Mother fed him some soup, and he fell asleep.

For several days, Alex did nothing more than sleep and eat. After two weeks, he could sit up in bed and was smiling. He was himself again. After six weeks, Father took the splints away from his legs. Father bent and rubbed his legs while he was still in bed and showed the rest of the family how to massage Alex's legs. Doing this would help him regain good circulation and increase the range of motion in his legs. It also helped rebuild some of the strength he had lost while he had lain in bed for six weeks. Everybody took turns helping Alex exercise his legs in bed before attempting to let him walk on them.

Helping Alex to exercise his legs became a pleasant household responsibility. We all took turns helping him until he was able to walk by himself. He was very independent. As he slowly started walking again, he would push us away and would not let us help him. He wanted to do it himself. However, after falling flat on his face once or twice, he realized that he needed help until his legs became stronger.

Subsequently, with encouragement from our parents and while holding onto his siblings, Alex began to walk. We encouraged him to start walking alone. Because of the falls, he was scared but eventually walked alone. Before long, Alex was not only walking but running by himself. His legs continued to get stronger all the time. He continued to develop normally with no residual effects to his entire body.

Chapter 20

Back to Kuldja

After moving back to Kuldja from Tugustaral, Father continued to look for work but was unable to find any. Then he heard that the town was looking for somebody who knew how to work with electricity. That immediately caught Father's attention. He knew electricity because he had worked with it. People who knew how to install and work with electricity were very scarce.

When Father went to inquire about the electrical job and whether it had been filled, Father told them he knew about electricity and had worked with it in Russia. The officials were very surprised and asked him to come and talk to them. They asked him to repair an electrical circuit where the light switch didn't work to see if he knew what he was doing. To their amazement, Father was able to repair and restore electrical power to that entire facility within minutes. They immediately hired him.

When he had been working there five days, two inspectors came to look at his work. They asked him questions about his work. They wanted to know where he had trained to do this quality of work. Father told them that he had learned how to work with electricity when he had lived on a farm. The farmer had shown him everything about electricity so he could help to restore all the electrical power on the farm when it was not working. After looking over all of the work that my father did, they said, "This is professional, quality work that you do. Keep up the good work."

When Father came to work the next morning, they told him that his services were no longer needed. They said that they had hired one of their own people that had come back to work for them. The former worker had been there previously and had done his job well until he had had to leave work for an unspecified amount of time due to an unexpected family illness. Now he was back. He was a good worker, and they knew him well. That was why they hired him back.

Father knew that the communists had forced the people to terminate his job. He recognized one of the inspectors. The man was not really an inspector but a communist, whom Father had seen many times before. This man was the one who ordered all the dirty work that was done by the communists. Father went home and prayed. Then he told his wife why he had been fired and that the communists were everywhere and would make it very difficult for them.

Father turned to other resources. Father built a small two-wheel cart for Tony's pony. Tony hauled coal from the mines. The miners would allow this thirteen-year-old lad to pick up small, discarded pieces of coal in the area. Tony collected all the coal pieces and put them in a sack on his cart.

Sometimes Tony took the coal straight to the main market and sold it, giving the money to Father to help support the family. Other times, he took it to the flea market to sell. He also brought part of it home to help heat the house. Sometimes, he was unable to sell all the coal. He then had to stay overnight in the market until the coal sold before he would come home.

The drive to the coal mine took about half a day. Tony would get up at one o'clock in the morning so he could arrive at the mine by sunup—the same time as the miners. On the way home, sometimes he would be so tired that he would fall asleep in his cart. When he woke up, the horse would be standing still.

At the mines, the coal miners had large baskets that they loaded onto their big wagons. It took two to three men to lift the basket into the wagon. The trip was always difficult, even when there were no problems. However, during the winter months, the roads were very muddy and were full of snow and ice. This made the work much more difficult for Tony. His small cart would become stuck many times in the mud, and his poor little horse was just not strong enough to pull the cart out of the mud. Thankfully, many passing coal miners would use their horses to pull Tony, his pony, and the cart out of the mud. This happened frequently in the winter months. Thank the Lord for those kindhearted people.

For several more months, Tony hauled coal from the mines to the market or sometimes to the house. Toward spring, the roads were clear and it was easier to haul the coal. After several weeks, everything seemed to be going quite well.

One day when he arrived at the mine very early, he found two men waiting for him. These two men were officials from the mine. These two men told him that all the land and the mines belonged to the government. They informed Tony that he was stealing coal from government property. If he continued to steal from the government, they would arrest him. The government (the communists) would put both him and his father in prison and would confiscate his horse and cart. Tony was very frightened.

As the officials walked away, Tony, with tears in his eyes, quickly got in his cart and rode home to tell Father the bad news. Upon arriving at the house, Tony explained to Father what had happened. Father told Tony not to worry. "We will pray and God will provide another opportunity for us as He always has in the past. We will continue to rely on God and not give in to communism."

Father told Tony that God would provide for the family. The next day, father took Tony's little cart and his small pony to the bazaar where he sold them and bought food for the family.

Because Father had refused to cooperate with the communists, he was denied a job everywhere he tried to apply. He knew that wherever he applied, he would face the same situation. Therefore, he knew that he would never get a job as long as the communists were in charge yet he remained strong in his faith and continued to resist them. However, Father knew that when one door closes, God opens another door.

Chapter 21

Making Combs

Father knew that in that part of the world, all the combs were made out of wood. They were weak and flimsy and broke easily. He decided to make combs out of animal horns. Father went to the police station to ask for permission to look through the rubble of the old bombed-out factory in town.

The police said, "Yeah, go ahead. We went through that blown-up plant and got everything that's usable out of there. There is nothing but junk there. But you're welcome to take from that junk anything you like. Take all of it and clean up the place for us. We won't mind a bit. Ha, ha, ha, ha, ha!" they laughed, as Father hurriedly headed for the bombed-out factory to look for things that he needed to create a comb-making machine.

He found a flat, circular, metallic disk. With very little to work with and with considerable difficulty, he made a hole in the center of the disk. The farmer, who had taken him in years before, had given him a small file as a going away present, saying, "Keep this in a safe place and always protected. It is a very useful tool, is very small, but it can do wonders."

Father remembered what the farmer had told him. He had been saving it for many years, and now the time had come for him to use it. He used the file to make small, sharp teeth in the circular, metallic disk. It was a painfully slow process, but he was very careful to make sure all the teeth on the circular disc were even, thus creating a circular saw blade.

He found a long metal rod in the bombed-out factory and was able to take it home with the blessing of the city officials. He mounted the circular blade on the rod and secured it. Next, he needed a pulley to attach to the rod and another pulley to attach to the foot pedal that would spin the saw blade.

Father searched the town and through the rubble of the destroyed buildings, especially the factories that had been destroyed by bombs. There he found a pulley, a belt, and another pulley still attached to a pedal from an old sewing machine. All of it was old, rusty, discarded junk, which the town hadn't wanted and didn't know what to do with.

After getting permission from the town officials again, he was allowed to take those old pieces from a bombed-out factory. The city officials called it "junk." Father took the "junk" home. He cleaned it up, attached it to the rod on his saw blade with the pulley, and attached the pulley to the bigger pulley, which was attached to the foot pedal. Now he could sit there and spin the blade as fast as his feet could pedal.

He needed a second rod, which had the thread on the outside of the entire length of it. He went back to the old factory and kept looking through the rubble for a second, threaded rod. He found it.

Now he had to go back to the authorities and ask permission to take the rod from the rubble. Again, the authorities looked at him and said, "Sure. Go ahead and take it. That factory is not usable. It is nothing but an eyesore for the town."

Father took the rod home, cleaned it up, and mounted it on his machine. On this threaded rod, he mounted a clamp to a horn plate so it wouldn't move. With the animal horn plate secured, he would pedal the footplate, which was attached to the circular saw by pulleys. The pulley would spin the circular blade. The animal horn plate was secured with the second rod and clamped at a predetermined distance from the spinning blade. The secured animal horn plate would be lowered onto the spinning blade, which would cut into the plate, thus creating teeth on the plate.

While Father was building his comb-making machine, he told all the kids to gather all the animal horns they could find from dead animal skulls in the desert and to bring them home. With his homemade circular saw, Father cut the longhorns into small pieces and then cut the pieces lengthwise in two. He heated each piece of horn and flattened it. He cut and flattened all the animal horns that the kids brought to him and carefully polished each piece to remove all the loose debris. Then he took a piece and locked it into his clamp, which was mounted on the threaded rod.

As he spun his circular saw, he lowered the clamped piece onto the rotating saw and made small teeth in the piece of horn. He made various sizes of combs: large combs, small combs with short teeth, and combs with long teeth. The combs with long teeth were wider with thicker teeth to give them more strength and to keep them from breaking easily.

People in that part of the world had coarse, long hair. The few wooden combs that they possessed had most of their teeth missing. They were just too fragile for the thick, coarse hair of the people. Father thought that combs made out of animal horns would be much stronger and more effective. These combs worked very well.

Father would make the combs at home, and Mother would take them and sell them. After buying one or two combs, the people were very pleased with the quality of the combs. The combs were very effective and did not break like their wooden combs did.

So our father was successful in making combs out of animal horns. It was a family project. The kids gathered the horns for Father. Father made combs out of the animal horns with his homemade comb-making machine. Mother sold the combs at the bazaar or traded them for meat (if and when it was available), cheese, butter, or material to make clothes for the family.

Chapter 22

George Hunter and the Russian People in Kuldja

Now there were many more Russian people in Kuldja, Xinjiang, China. Among them there were many Christian believers as a result of George Hunter's previous years of ministry. George Hunter was a Scottish Protestant missionary who played a vital role in our journey to America.

George Hunter spent fifty years of his life doing missionary work in northwestern China. He spent most of his time in Xinjiang Province and the Gobi Desert. During his time in Xinjiang (Sinkiang) Province, he traveled widely, preaching in multiple local ethnic languages, such as Kazakh, Uyghur, Manchu, Mongolian, Nogai, Arabic, and Chinese. He also distributed literature in those languages. His main desire was to bring the unsaved to Christ, especially the Muslim people. Hunter also translated parts of the New Testament and Old Testament and the book, *Pilgrim's Progress*, into local languages.

In Kuldja, George Hunter encountered a small community of Russians. During his travels, he frequently visited Kuldja to work with the small group of Russian people that was there and to encourage them spiritually, leaving his mark on the Russian community.

George Hunter was arrested under false charges during Shang Shicai's reign in Xinjiang, China, and was locked up in a soviet prison in Urumqi, Xinjiang, for thirteen months. During the time of his imprisonment, he was subjected to various tortures for his faith. He never renounced Christ but remained faithful throughout his imprisonment. At the request of the British government, George Hunter was released from prison and escorted out of the city. It is my understanding that the Muslims and the communists banned him from doing missionary work in Urumqi and the entire province of Xinjiang.

After being released from prison, George Hunter continued to do God's work in northern Gansu Province, southwestern Mongolia, and the Gobi Desert instead of Xinjiang (Sinkiang) Province. While in Gansu Province, he spent many hours gazing westward across the border into Sinkiang Province. He prayed that someday soon the province would open its doors to him so he could go back and continue ministering to the Muslim people.

A small group of believers had emerged as a result of his witnessing to the Russian people in Kuldja. The group organized and became a church.

12. Photo of George Hunter, Protestant
Christian missionary from Scotland

George Hunter, was imprisoned for thirteen months in Urumqi and then was released and banished by the communists and the Muslims from doing missionary work in Urumqi and the entire province of Xinjiang (Sinkiang). The small Russian group of believers in Kuldja carried on. The communists were constantly harassing them. After George Hunter had been banished from the Xinjiang province, there was no fully ordained minister to take his place to help the Russian believers in Kuldja. However, they struggled without giving up hope.

Father was asked to step in and help. He was ordained and had much experience dealing with the communists in Russia. He knew who and what he was against—the communists! His position did not last long. The communists came with full force and took over all of Sinkiang Province. Father's military friends warned him that the communists in Kuldja were after him. Father, once again, made the wise decision to leave Kuldja, this time permanently.

13. A Street in Urumqi

Chapter 23

Renounce God, Embrace Communism, and Live

Upon arriving in Kuldja from Russia, Father had difficulty finding work of any kind because of his strong faith and refusal to cooperate with the communists. During these initial years in Kuldja when there were frequent struggles for power, Father would move the family temporarily away from the city until things settled down. Then he would move the family back to Kuldja. Father did this to avoid direct conflict with the communists.

When things appeared to be fairly quiet in the town, Father would start looking for work, but as usual, when they found out that he was a strong believer in God and preached against communism, he was denied work.

He was told that if he would cooperate with the communists, he could get any job for life. He would also have lifetime security for his family and for himself. All he had to do was renounce God and embrace communism. It was such a simple request, but what a price one had to pay for it!

In 1945, the communists became more aggressive. They would come across the border at night from Russia. They would stir up trouble between the Russian, Chinese, Dunganese, Muslims, and the other ethnic groups in the area. Then they would disappear. They continued using these tactics repeatedly. They got all the ethnic groups fighting each other. Then they would come across the border in force and would say that they were there to rescue the oppressed Russian people from all the other ethnic groups.

They took over the entire province of Xinjiang, China. After this, there was much more bloodshed in the province. Fierce fighting took place everywhere. People were slaughtered like animals!

Xinjiang Province is one of China's richest natural resource areas. The battle for control and independence of Xinjiang Uygurt Province continues to rage on to this day.

Chapter 24

Communists Driven Back to Russia

Finally, the Chinese overpowered the communists. They drove them out of Xinjiang (Sinkiang) Province back across the border into Russia. Shortly after the communists were driven back to Russia, one of my father's old friends from the Chinese army came to see him. He told my father that after they had chased the communists out of the police station and across the border, they had found many documents in the police station. Some of these documents had contained blacklists of the people to be executed for treason or for talking against the communists.

He said, "Peter, your name was at the top of the list. They must want you badly. I talked to many of my friends who know you, and they said for me to tell you to be very careful. The communists want you dead for some reason."

Father thanked his friend for warning him. He didn't say anything to anybody but continued to minister at the church. In the meantime, he quietly started building a two-wheeled cart. People would go by the house where we lived and say, "Look at that crazy man building a two-wheeled cart. Where does he expect to go on a homemade two-wheeled cart? We're in the middle of a war zone. Beyond the war zone lies one of worst desert wastelands of the world, the Taklamakan Desert and the Gobi Desert. This is the time to stay home and pray to God that we may be spared and the communists don't take over the country completely. It is too dangerous to travel! Besides it's in the late summer and already getting cold. Fall and winter are rapidly approaching. From the looks of things, this winter is going to be very harsh."

The word spread through town that Father was building a two-wheeled cart. "He only has one small horse. How does he expect the small horse to pull the cart? He and his wife have eight children, ranging in age from five months to fifteen years. Where will they put the babies? This is too much to even think about. He won't get too far outside of town before his whole family is killed. If they survive the war zone, then they will surely die in the wastelands of the Gobi Desert. What is this crazy man thinking?"

His church members told him, "This is suicide to try to go anywhere now. You will all die. It is too dangerous out there."

But Father did not disagree or argue with anybody. He simply would say, "Yeah, yeah." He would smile, nod his head in agreement, and continue working on his two-wheeled cart. He completed the cart but did not assemble it. That way, people would think that he did not know how to finish it.

Chapter 25

Xinjiang (Sinkiang) Province Now Under Full Communist Control

Several months went by, and the communists attacked again. This time they were very forceful and took over the entire province of Xinjiang (Sinkiang), China. Now the communists were in full control of the entire province. The communists restricted people from going from one town to another. They had roadblocks and checkpoints everywhere.

Then the roadblocks and checkpoints were removed. They would not allow social gatherings. Then they started checking people by going to each house's door. They wanted to know who lived there. How many people were in the house? What type of citizenship did they have, Russian or Chinese? They also wanted to know what kind of passport each person had.

One day, they arrived at our house and were asking Father many questions. How many people lived in his house? My father was asked what kind of passports he and his wife had. My father told them that he and his wife had Chinese passports. They had all the Chinese documents to be in the country legally. Father told them that they had lived in China for about fifteen years.

They asked him again why a Russian man with a Russian family would have a Chinese passport. My father replied, "Because my family and I live in China, and we need our Chinese documents." When the questioning was over, the two men turned around and quickly walked out.

After the two men left the house, my father told us that we must prepare to leave right away. He told us not to say anything to anybody. Father had anticipated this situation and was already preparing for it.

Chapter 26

Getting Ready to Flee

Before fleeing Kuldja, Father and Mother prepared for the journey without telling the kids about it. We knew that something was different but didn't know what. Father sent us out every day looking for horns or animal skulls with horns. He instructed, "Make sure you visit all the meat markets and slaughterhouses and collect all the horns and skulls from them. Bring all the horns home. It does not matter if they are small horns, large horns, or half a horn. Bring them all just the same." We knew Father made combs that were in demand. Now Father was almost forceful when he told us to search every day for the horns.

"Try not to come back without skulls or horns. Get in the habit of always bringing something home. Never come back empty-handed. Don't come back without any horns. Bring us skulls with horns or just horns by themselves if you can." We never questioned Father. We did what he told us to do.

The past several weeks, Father had made many combs. The combs that he made were all different sizes and shapes. From the little horns that we brought him, Father made small combs. He made many more combs than usual. We noticed that Mother was not selling them like she normally did, but we didn't think much about it. We continued bringing all the horns we could find, with or without the skull. Father kept making combs and putting them away instead of selling them at the marketplace.

Father was making the combs and was saving them to take with us on our journey. When the time came for us to leave, he took all the combs that he made and wrapped them individually. If he had wrapped them into one large bundle, it would have been obvious that something of value was wrapped and protected with cloth. Combs did not take much room, so to throw off the suspicions of the communists in case we were stopped and searched, he wrapped them individually and scattered them all over the cart. Some he even stuck in between two sacks on the floor of the cart. He used dirty rags, pieces of cloth, or anything he could find to protect the combs as much as possible. If they were to detect a bundle of combs wrapped and tucked away, they could have confiscated all of them. Then they would have arrested Father for transporting contraband. He would immediately end up in a Siberian prison facing execution.

In the meantime, Mother was also preparing for the journey. She made lots of bread, sliced it, dried it, and placed it into sacks. Dried, sliced, bread was the same as crackers—it would last a long time without spoiling.

After Father made enough combs for the journey, he quickly took the comb-making machine to the bazaar and exchanged it for a big horse. He said that in order for us to travel we needed two horses. The man at the bazaar did not want his horse because the horse had a big, open, draining wound on his neck. Father looked at the horse and realized that it was very healthy, strong, and big. He thought he knew how to doctor this infection. The man wanted Father's comb-making machine, so Father exchanged his machine for the horse. We could not take the comb-making machine with us so we would have to leave it there anyway. Both men were very happy. They both got what they wanted.

Now that we had two horses, Father put all of his energy into finishing the two-wheeled cart. People continued to make fun of him, but he ignored them and kept working on the cart. About a week later, he finished the cart.

First of all, Father took the many combs that he had made for the trip and distributed them all over the floor of the cart. He wrapped them individually in any small rags he could find. He placed other combs between sacks or anywhere they would fit. In case we were caught, they wouldn't confiscate all the combs.

Then we put aside all of our belongings that we needed for the journey. We packed several sacks of dried bread for the trip that Mother had been preparing for quite some time. The dried bread would also be scattered throughout the cart. We prepared and saved feed for the horses.

When we completed loading the cart, mother had Tava, Tony, and Benny help her clean the house. After it was cleaned, we gathered together in the empty house, took off our hats, and prayed. Father prayed for a safe journey, wherever we were going, and most of all, that God's will would be fulfilled in all of this.

Father put Mother and Nikki in the cart. The rest of us walked behind the cart. Just as we started, our Muslim neighbor lady came and gave us a big stack of flatbread for the journey, saying, "Take this. You will need this food as you travel. May Allah go with you and give you a safe journey." Because of all the turmoil and killing in town, nobody else came out to say goodbye. All of our church members were afraid to come because they were being watched very closely by the communists.

My father said that the communists had completely taken over Russia. They had executed all the former leaders of Russia and all the Christians that opposed communism and the belief in a utopia for all mankind, which would be established by the communists. Now the communists were in northwestern China.

Their first attempt to take over Xinjiang Province, China, failed. The second red wave from the north was much more powerful, and they had succeeded in taking over the entire province. They were systematically taking control of every major town in the province and eliminating all opposition, including all those that preached about God and salvation through the Lord Jesus Christ as their personal Savior (John 14:6).

According to the communists, there was only one God and that was communism. Therefore, their main goal was to eradicate all opposition against communism. According to Lenin and Stalin, the Bible and religion were like opium or poison, which corrupted the mind and turned the people against the true faith—communism. They preached communism as the future utopia and the supreme authority for all people.

Father knew that communism was not a utopia. It was nothing more than brainwashing people's minds and enslaving them for the rest of their lives. Their philosophy of people was similar to that of the farmer and his animals: Communist philosophy stated that once a person was nonproductive and began to be dependent on other people, he caused a drain and a strain on the people around him. Therefore, just like a nonproductive farm animal, he must be eliminated for the good of the society. No work, no food.

Stalin used small, hungry children as an example to prove to all the other little children that communism was the supreme authority over all people. He placed these children around a big table. He said to them, "Children, let us close our eyes and pray to God to give us food because we are hungry." All the children closed their eyes and prayed, and when they had finished praying, they opened their eyes and noted that there was no food on the table. Then Stalin said, "Let us pray to communism to give us food because we are hungry." So once again, the children closed their eyes and prayed this time to communism. While the children were praying, the communists brought large portions of food to the children and placed them on the table in front of them. Now Stalin said, "You see who brought the food to you? Your God to whom you prayed or communism, the supreme god of mankind? Yes. You see and know who the real god is. Yes, it has to be the one that brought you the good food. Children, you must never forget that communism is the supreme god of mankind."

Today in Russia, Putin, like Stalin, Kruschev, and other predecessors, is using the same communist tactics and methods! People would disappear at night, and nobody knew what happened to them. Similarly in the Ukraine today, Russian soldiers supposedly were sent for a simple, routine, two-week training exercise somewhere in Russia. Ironically, very few returned alive! They were not told that they were going to the

Ukraine to fight a war. They were simply told that they were going on a two-week military training exercise in Russia!

Parents of the missing soldiers in Russia are organizing and demanding answers. They are asking questions. They say, "Our sons went on a two-week military maneuver in Russia. Now it is a year that our sons have been gone. We have had no word from them. What kind of maneuvers did they go on? We want our sons back. Are they alive? If not, we want to know how they died and where they died. If they are dead, we want to see their bodies. We want the bodies brought home so we can bury them. If this was simply a field exercise, why are all these soldiers being killed?

These are the questions that Putin is facing now. These questions are hard for him to answer because he has been cremating most of the soldiers who were killed in the Ukraine. Soon the truth about Putin's shenanigans in the Ukraine will be public knowledge worldwide. God will deal with Mr. Putin when the time comes.

This is why Father prayed to God for wisdom and guidance. He prayed to God to be delivered from the deadly grip of communism. If he was not delivered from the grip of communism, it would subsequently lead him to his death by execution.

Father knew what the real intentions were. Therefore, he said that we must leave this part of the country to escape the deadly grip of communism. Father had eluded capture by the communists many times in the province of Siberia in Russia. They were furious that he had escaped all the traps in Russia. Now they were more determined than ever to get him. He was a marked man, and execution inevitably awaited him upon his capture.

Father said that eventually, all of China would be under communist control, so we had to leave that part of the country before it was too late. They eventually would close all the borders and nobody would be allowed to leave. We could not worship God there, just as in Russia, and so we had to leave and find a free country where we could worship God.

Chapter 27

Fleeing Kuldja

We left Kuldja in the middle of the night to attract as little attention as possible and to travel as far as we could under the cover and protection of darkness. As we left the town, we continued to walk in the dark, always following our father, who was leading with the cart. He knew where he was going, but we did not. So we just followed him in the dark, trailing behind the cart.

After walking the remainder of the night, we saw dawn creep over the horizon in front of us while the shadows of the night receded behind us, leaving us exposed and vulnerable. We tried to stay in the darkness as long as possible, not wanting to be exposed by daylight. Daylight meant we might be captured and killed. Our lives might instantly be snuffed out.

We felt as if we were night blooming flowers. Once the sunlight hits them, they immediately start to wither, dry up, and disappear. It almost seemed as if the darkness was clinging to the ground around us and was refusing to dissipate, so we would not be exposed by the light. As we continued to walk, the darkness around us was slowly loosening its grip. We witnessed the transformation of darkness to a grayish-blue haze, which intermingled with the white rays of light breaking across the horizon in front of us

It was becoming daylight. We looked around. Now that we could see the countryside around us, we saw many dead people along the side of the road. Some of them were partially covered with dirt and others were not. Sometimes we saw an arm sticking out of the ground, and sometimes a head on the ground. Many bodies were lying beside the road uncovered. Quickly and quietly, we walked behind the cart, holding each other's hands so we wouldn't get separated.

Father said that these people had been killed recently. "We must walk quickly and quietly away from these killing fields before it gets too light. It is very dangerous here. If they catch us, they'll probably kill us. We must leave this area as quickly as we can. It is daylight. We must find a place to hide and rest for the day. When it gets dark, we will start walking again."

At this point Mother started to cry and said, "Let's go back into town where it is safe! It is too dangerous out here. We will all be killed! The people in our church were right. It is too dangerous out here. We must go back into town before it's too late."

Father came to the back of the cart where all of us were standing and crying. Mother was sitting on top of the cart with the baby in her arms. She was crying as well, saying, "I don't want to die. Let's go back into town where it is safe."

While all of us stood close to each other, Father said, "Let us pray again, and pray that we are doing the right thing. It is very dangerous out here, and we must let God guide us where He wants us to go. It is His will that we must fulfill."

After praying, we all felt uplifted. Father smiled, looked up at mother, and in his usual soft voice said to her, "Now that we have rested, we must go on." With our spirits uplifted and physical strength renewed (Isaiah 40:30–31), we all agreed that we needed to move quickly forward. We knew that going back would mean certain death for our father.

In the midst of the horrible death scenes surrounding us, we followed the cart, carefully avoiding the exposed bodies on the road. As we continued to walk briskly, we would occasionally glance quickly at the bodies on the road and those that were pulled off the roads. Most of the bodies that we saw were partially covered with dirt and had very few clothes on them. Apparently, somebody had come and stripped all the outer garments that were of value off most of the bodies.

The smell of death was everywhere. We hurriedly walked behind the cart and were preoccupied with trying our best not to step on any of the bodies on the road in front of us. In the midst of all of this, Mother was gripped with fear. She started crying again as she clung tightly to little Nikki in her arms. As she continued crying, she kept on asking if they were doing the right thing.

"Maybe we need to go back into town where it is safe," she repeated.

Father, always with a gentle tone in his soft voice, would say, "God will guide and help us through this difficult part of our journey."

As we left Kuldja behind and walked through the killing fields, we walked every night for many weeks and hid during the day. Traveling southeast toward the rising sun, we saw the big mountains in the distance to the left of us. Father continued to go southeast parallel to the mountains. As dawn crept over the mountains on the left, we went into hiding. We rested during the day and waited for darkness to fall— that was our cue to start walking again.

Now that we were traveling in the more remote areas of China, we continued our journey. At times, Father would leave the family and go by himself searching for water and food. He would always bring something back to us. Many times, we were forced to journey during the day searching for water, which we desperately needed for both ourselves and the horses. Traveling at night, we had difficulty finding any wells along the road in the darkness. In order to see the wells, we had to travel by day. This was very dangerous for us, but we had no choice. Without water we would all die.

One day while searching for water on our desert journey, we finally saw a well in the distance. We were so thankful that now we would finally get some water for the horses and us. Some of the wells in the desert had a steep stairway, which began some distance away from the well and had steps going all the way down to the water level. That way, people who did not have any ropes could walk down, fill their buckets, and walk up again.

We were very familiar with this type of desert well. When Father walked down the narrow pathway to the bottom of the well, however, he hurriedly came back up the stairs with a fearful look on his face. He exclaimed, "We must leave here right away! There's no water in this well. The communists were here. They killed many people and threw their bodies into the well. There's nothing in this well except human bodies." This explained why there were no people around the well.

"We must keep going. It is too dangerous here! Many people died here, maybe yesterday, or maybe two days ago. The bodies are still fresh and do not smell yet. The communists must be close by here somewhere. We must quickly leave and find another well, maybe another day's walk from here. We can't stop here. We must get away from here as quickly as we can and search for another well with water in it instead of bodies."

After journeying another day, we finally found a well with fresh water. There were many people around the well. There were individual travelers on camels as well as camel caravans. They all wanted water from the well. With the help of some camel drivers, we hurriedly got water for our horses and ourselves and left the area. Father knew the communists patrolled this area. He wanted to get his family away from there as quickly as possible.

As we continued on from there, we approached a small village where we stopped. We were detained for three days while the authorities questioned our family with Chinese documents.

We needed corn for the horses and food and water for ourselves but had no money. However, Father was prepared for this moment. The bottom of our cart was covered with the combs Father had made out of animal horns. As we approached a village, we exchanged our combs for food, water, and corn. The combs, as the saying goes, were our bread and butter on our journey. Without those combs that Father had made in Kuldja, we probably would have died from dehydration and starvation in the Gobi Desert. Once the local people tried my father's combs, which were much stronger than wooden ones, they immediately liked them and wanted more. They worked better, did not break, and lasted longer than wooden combs.

We continued pushing deeper into the Gobi Desert. One day as we neared another settlement, for some reason Father was very apprehensive about this village. Something told him not to go into the village but to go around it. So Father said, "We must go around this village to avoid being captured by the communists here." We bypassed it and headed toward the hills.

As we approached the hills, the sun crept over the distant mountains. The hills looked very big, but the mountains looked even larger. On the other side of the village, we picked up the trail again and began to follow it into the hills. Once more, we slowly but steadily resumed our walk on the narrow road paralleling the foothills and the big mountains to our left. We continued to go which led us closer to the foothills. Here the ground was more solid, making it easier for the horses to pull the cart and for us to walk faster. The moon was bright, traveling was easy, and as a result, we made good time that night.

We began looking for a place away from the road to hide for the day, as we dared not be seen on the road in the daytime. Here we encountered more bodies along the road. Father admonished, "Don't look down. Just look straight ahead and walk behind us." Even though Father said not to look, who could resist looking? Some of the bodies were partially covered with dirt and others were not covered at all. Some places we would see an arm, a leg, or a head sticking out.

We were very frightened. Scared and emotional, Mother started crying. Then the infant in her arms started crying. Now the rest of us were on the verge of crying. Father stopped the horses and came to the back where Mother and the children were. He saw that they were all very frightened and crying. He said, "It is very dangerous here. But it would be worse if we went back. Here we still have a fighting chance to survive and live."

Father again urged us to pray, saying, "Let's pray that God's will is done. If it is His will that we die here, then His will shall be fulfilled. It shall be so."

Mother wanted to go back into town where it was safer. However, Father, in his usual soft voice insisted, "We must go on. We must leave this part of the country and go where it is safe to live." We all trusted and followed Father southeast into the desert and continued our journey for several weeks, still traveling at night and hiding during the day.

We feared the communists would find us and make us turn back. The communists supposedly had given a *window of opportunity* for all the people who wanted to leave this part of the country. It meant that all the Chinese people who did not want to stay were allowed to leave, but as usual, the communists did not hold to their promise. The window of opportunity conveniently closed. Maybe this window of opportunity did not exist to begin with?

Now all the people were asked to stay or leave their things behind when they went. Those who refused to leave were executed in their homes. Others were stripped of all their belongings or their good clothes and were loaded on wagons, taken into the mountains, and left to freeze to death. The communists told them to take only the things they could carry and nothing more. They were to leave their homes, furniture, horses, wagons, and everything else that they owned. Those who refused to go were executed immediately. We heard testimonials from many people who were fleeing from Sinkiang Province. Of course, this was nothing new for Father. He had expected this and had wanted to leave before something worse had happened.

The communists were very interested in catching all the Russian people, especially Christians who preached against communism. They wanted to send them back to Russia and to deal with them more permanently. Father anticipated this, and that was the reason we were traveling at night and hiding during the day. He knew that if they caught us, they would send us to Russian Siberian labor camps and death. This was the reason why we avoided going through Urumqi, the communist stronghold. Urumqi was where George Hunter was imprisoned for thirteen months. Father was well aware of this.

At the last village, we had been detained for three days waiting for our papers before we were allowed to continue traveling to the next village. Being detained while waiting for documents was almost a weekly occurrence. This happened four days before we reached Urumqi. The headman of the village told us to go straight to Urumqi to get more help and directions. Father knew better. He was very nice to the headman and even asked for directions to Urumqi.

As soon as we left the village, however, Father did not follow the directions the headman had given him. Instead, he went southeast away from Urumqi. Father knew that if we went to Urumqi, it would be the end of our journey. We continued to make our way southeast in the foothills, staying clear of the sand dunes to the right and the tall mountains to the left. We were traveling on foot with no roads to guide us.

After traveling seven more nights, we met a Russian speaking man who whistled happily as he walked at night in the opposite direction. He said that he was going up north about two nights' walk from there to visit his family and relatives.

He told my father, "Continue in the same direction as you're going now for three more nights. Then on the fourth night, you will cross a highway. Make a left turn onto the highway and go for three more nights. The road will be smooth, and the horses will walk much faster and cover a lot of territory in three nights on the highway.

"After the third night, look for a big curve in the road. You must get off the highway at that point, because at the other end of the big curve, there is a guard station and a communist checkpoint. You must get off the highway before then. If you do not, you will be caught and either executed or taken back to Russia and put in prison. So be alert, the third night is when you have to be extra careful and watch for the curve in the road. You do not want to miss the curve in the road because your life depends on it."

Father thanked the man graciously for the directions and the advice. The man continued walking north, and we continued walking south.

Chapter 28

Communist Checkpoint

After walking three nights, we started looking for the highway but did not see it. On the fourth night, we found it. Father immediately started traveling on it. Like the man had said, it was very easy going. The horses pulled the cart without difficulty, but we had a hard time keeping up with the horses. Several times when we encountered the headlights of a vehicle on the highway coming toward us, Father quickly got the horses off the highway, and we hid in the bushes. When everything was dark and quiet again, Father would lead us back on the highway, and we would continue.

In the middle of our third night on the highway, Father said, "Tomorrow, early in the evening, we must look for the big curve in the road. That will be our sign to get off the highway and travel for one night around the curve to avoid the communist checkpoint."

No sooner had Father finished saying this than we were surrounded by bright lights from every direction and Chinese soldiers with guns. They gave the command in Chinese and Russian to stop and raise our hands. They did not talk much but just spoke in Chinese among themselves. Apparently, the commander told the soldiers in Chinese to line us up and shoot us. Father knew that the Chinese commander understood and spoke Russian, but he insisted on speaking in Chinese. We were told through a translator that we were traveling illegally on a highway that was built for cars and trucks only. Horses and wagons were forbidden on this highway.

We were lined up to be executed. At about this time, one of the soldiers came running up to the commander and pointed at his gun while speaking Chinese. All the other soldiers nodded their heads as they talked to each other and to the commander. There appeared to be some confusion in the group.

Mother took advantage of this. She ran up to the commander, fell on her knees in front of him, and pleaded for the lives of our family, "For the sake of our crippled little boy, who cannot walk, please spare our lives." She began to cry and beg for our lives.

At that moment, out of the shadows of the night, three hunters appeared and joined the group of soldiers. They seemed to know each other well. They were happy and cheerful, carrying on with each other as if they were old friends. The commander appeared to know them as well. He joined the friendly conversation with the hunters.

The hunters also pointed to their guns, and the consensus was that majority of the guns were not functioning. The hunters asked the soldiers if they could fix their guns, but the soldiers said no. Then the commander looked at my father and asked, "Do you know how to fix guns?" The commander understood and spoke Russian. Father was not surprised—most of the soldiers, especially the officers who were trained by the communists, were also taught Russian.

He looked at my father and again asked, "Can you fix guns?"

My father responded, "Yes, I can fix guns."

Then the commander gave my father one of the broken guns and ordered, "You fix gun now." Father took the gun, checked it carefully, cleaned it, repaired it, and gave it back to the commander. One by one, Father fixed all the broken guns for the soldiers and the hunters. When he had restored all the guns to working order and had given them back, the soldiers and the hunters were very happy.

They started joking, laughing, and rolling their own cigarettes. The commander joined in the fun as one of the soldiers rolled a cigarette, lit it, puffed on it a couple of times to make sure it was burning, and gave it to his commander. This pleased the commander, as it made him look very important in front of everybody.

The commander would exchange a few words with the soldier who gave him the cigarette. Then the two started to speak in Chinese with the rest of the group. They continued to converse in Chinese and occasionally would throw an unexpected glance in our direction. They pointed at us, still lined up to be executed. Mother, along with all the little children, was crying. We waited for and dreaded that one final order the commander would give, "Execute them." Then we would be killed instantly by the same guns that Father had repaired for them.

They continued to laugh and joke while casting a casual glance in our direction, knowing quite well that we did not speak or understand Chinese. After what appeared to be an eternity of waiting, the commander and the hunters came up to us. The commander looked at my mother, who was crying and holding her seven-month-old infant.

My leg had been paralyzed from infancy. I was unable to walk or stand well. Therefore, I was sitting on the ground next to Mother clutching tightly to her leg. The commander looked at me and then at Father and the rest of the children and said, "Because you have helped us so much and helped our friends the hunters, all of us decided to spare your lives. You must leave here right away before the other soldiers with the new commander come here to replace us. They will not let you go. They will execute you here. You must not travel on the highway again. If they catch you again, they surely will execute all of you. Now, go quickly. Get off the highway and don't come back!"

We immediately left the checkpoint and vanished into the dark night before they changed their minds. All of us were very much surprised when they told us that they were not going to kill us. Father said he didn't know whether they were going to shoot us in the back or actually let us go. While we were still within earshot of the soldiers and with the lights shining on our backs, Father said, "Tony, pick up little George and carry him so we can run faster. We must get away from here as quickly as we can while we are still alive!"

Tony grabbed me, threw me on his back, and ran with me. We were all very frightened, not knowing whether we were going to get out of there alive or get shot in the back trying to escape. Was this the end of our journey? Maybe we were destined to die out there in the desert.

Once we were far enough away, we could not see the lights behind us anymore or hear the soldiers' voices. The silence and darkness enveloped us. Father said, "Let us stop here and pray." As we removed our hats and prayed, Father thanked God for bringing us safely through the dangerous incident we had just faced. We had survived with God's help and guidance. We were very grateful for the safety of our family thus far on our long journey. He closed the prayer by asking that God's will would be done in everything that we did.

After our prayer, we moved rapidly across the open fields to get as far and as fast as we could from the checkpoints. Father didn't think about the directions anymore. He just wanted to get away from the communist checkpoint as quickly as possible. It was still hard for us to believe that they had let us go.

Tony kept carrying me on his back. Occasionally, I would slowly slip down off his back and find myself being dragged by Tony's strong hand. I didn't complain. I just kept moving as fast as I could, but apparently I was not fast enough. Tony would pick me up again and put me on his shoulders so I was not slowing the group down.

We continued walking across the countryside the rest of the night. The moon was out, and we felt like walking because we were under pressure to get away from there. Besides, it was a very warm night. Toward daybreak, we were all exhausted. The fields we were crossing were covered with rocks and animal holes. This made walking at night very difficult and perilous, especially for those in a hurry, trying to escape from somebody attempting to kill them.

Father said we had been walking across the fields for hours. We all were at the point of exhaustion. We needed to stop and rest. Besides, it was early dawn and time for us to find a hiding place to rest for the day. We would travel again at night when it was safer and cooler.

We noticed that as the dawn crept over the horizon, it was already getting warmer. In the early morning light, we could see the desolate countryside with its parched, dry ground and no vegetation as far as the eye could see. We were traveling in the Turpan Basin—the hottest and the lowest region in China!

Chapter 29

The Village of Turpan

(The Old Name Was Turfan)

After traveling several nights past the checkpoint, we came to a small village called Turpan (Turfan). Turpan is 505 feet below sea level and is the lowest and hottest place in China. Death Valley in Mojave desert is 282 feet below sea level and is the lowest and hottest area in the United States.

As we approached the village, Father said that we must stop on the outskirts of the village while he went in to ask for our traveling papers to go to the next town or if we could go to the next town without papers. He knew it was a communist village because there was a small red flag flying on top of one of the buildings. Father went into the village and showed them our documents to get permission and travel papers for the next village. Some of the villagers spoke Russian and some spoke Arabic, so Tava and Tony went with Father.

Father told the headman that we must go to the next village to visit some relatives. The headman asked, "Why you want to go there?"

"We have relatives there, and one of their family members there is very sick."

"I will see about getting papers for you to go to the next village."

In the meantime, the headman sent three soldiers with red armbands to our cart outside the village to see what we had. The soldiers walked around the cart and looked at it and the old horses. With their rifles pointed at mother, they ordered her and the infant off the cart. Then the soldiers plunged their bayonets into our bundles of clothes on the cart to make sure we were not hiding something of value. They took some of the clothes bundles and threw them on the ground.

One of the soldiers picked up a bundle off the cart, looked at it, and dropped it right away. Telling the other soldiers to back away and not touch it, he said "They're infested. Don't touch their clothes." He motioned for the kids to pick up the clothes and the bundles and put them back in the cart.

The soldier kept looking at his hands, trying to brush something off them. He kept motioning with his bayonet for the boys to pick up the clothes and put them back on the cart. The other soldiers took several steps back, moving away from the cart and from the clothes. We didn't know what was going on because they were speaking Chinese. Later, we found out they were saying we were diseased.

All the clothes that we had in the cart and on us were covered with fleas and lice. They hurried back to the village and told the headman what they had found. The headman said to my father, "You have eight children. You must be careful to take good care of them. Here are your papers to go to the next village. You and your family can go now. Don't go through the village. You must go around the village."

Father asked him how far it was to the next village. The man said, "Follow that road, and you will reach it in about fifteen to twenty days walking." Because we feared being captured by the communists, we walked by night and avoided the road.

Chapter 30

The Village of Hami (Kumul)

The village of Hami was the last village in communist China before crossing into free China. A permanent red army unit (8th regiment) was established in Hami to protect the border from invaders from Mongolia. The communist regiment was present but the locals were still in charge. The red army unit was more concerned with invaders from the north. They were not as concerned with the refugees fleeing the country.

We followed the road as the headman had told us to, heading southeast. After about eighteen days of walking, we reached the edge of the village of Hami and stopped. We were cold, exhausted, hungry, and thirsty. We sat on the side of the road while Father went inside to talk to the officials. He was gone for a long time. Then he returned with several officials, who came out to see how we were traveling.

They walked around the cart and then looked up and saw Mother sitting on top of the cart with the seven month old in her arms. They looked at the other seven kids sitting on the side of the road. They carefully looked at the horses before backing away.

Apparently, they were disappointed. They probably hoped to see some healthy-looking horses instead of half-dead animals. One small horse was old and nothing but skin and bones. The other horse was large but also very skinny and had a big, open, draining abscess on his neck. They kept pointing and looking at the one with the large open wound.

They shook their heads in disbelief and walked away. We evidently had nothing of value that they wanted.

We sat there on the side of the road waiting for Father to come back from the meeting with the officials. A Muslim lady came out from the village carrying lots of flatbread. She gave it to Mother, saying, "Feed the children! This bread will be your food while traveling." She added that she had overheard the men talking inside. "They said that you are too much trouble. They want you to leave as quickly as you can. They said that you had two sick old horses and eight small children. They said that you are a bad omen for this village. They will give you your papers and want you to leave right away.

"The men in the village said that you must go around the village. They don't want you to infect the villagers or their animals. They said you have very sick horses. You must not go through the village.

"I wanted to come and see the children before you left. I wanted to bring the children some food and water. You must be very careful traveling here. There are many bad people here outside the village. They will kill you if they catch you off guard!

"After seven to eight days of walking in that direction," she pointed east, "you will cross the river bridge into free China. After crossing the river bridge, you will be much safer. That is the free China on the other side of the river. But you must be very careful. There are many communists here. Here you must travel at night to be safe from the communists.

"Five days from today, you may start traveling in the daytime and meet wagon trains going in the same direction as you will be going. They also are fleeing from communism. The communists are giving these people the last chance to leave this territory before they will close all the borders. They will be crossing the river to free China. This is where you must cross with them to be safe. Go with them and it will be safer for you. The communists are allowing only the people with Chinese documents to leave. We heard that they will close all the borders very soon and nobody will be able to leave communist China.

"I must go now. May Allah go with you and protect you."

No sooner had the lady walked away from us than a man came carrying our papers. He said that the headman and the village council decided to let us go.

He said, "You must leave tonight! Tomorrow the communist soldiers will stand guard here and they may not let you pass! The communist soldiers, when they are not drunk, stop all the Russian people and turn them back, but when they are drunk and are on duty here, they don't care! Everybody is allowed to pass!"

Father said he understood and thanked the man for giving us the papers to travel. The travel papers were our Chinese documents that Father had refused to surrender to the communists in Kuldja, China. The man emphasized strongly that we must leave immediately. He said it was good that we had Chinese documents, not Russian documents.

He said, "If you had Russian documents, we would not allow you to go past this village. You would be forced to turn around and go back." He added, "If you value your lives, you will go around the village, not through it."

As soon as we saw the man leave, Father got our things together and walking away from the village. After putting some distance between us and the village during the night, we stopped to pray, thanking God that we had not been detained in the village. According to the lady, we were only about eight nights of walking away from the free China border. We had to be extra careful not to get caught by the communists this close to free China. After five more nights of walking, we would join the wagon train leaving communist China. Then we would travel during the day with the wagon train and be much safer.

After walking briskly most of the night, we were very tired, cold, and hungry and really welcomed the flatbread that the lady had given us. Father rationed out a piece of flatbread to each child. Then he gave one to his wife and took one for himself.

We kept a rapid pace throughout the night. The moon was shining brightly, and the ground was flat and firm, making easy traveling for the horses. We had a little trouble keeping up with the horses, as they were pulling the cart with ease.

The man and the lady from the village had told us we could start traveling safely during the day after we joined the wagon train. Soon we would only be three days away from the border that separated free China from communist China. There would be many people traveling in the same direction. Therefore, we would be safe from bandits who attacked people on the road. All the people with proper Chinese papers would be allowed to enter free China. There was a big bridge across the river, and once we crossed over the bridge, we would be in free China and safe from the communists.

Everybody felt good after praying and eating the flatbread. We had more energy to walk. By the next morning, we began to see some people walking in the same direction. We tagged along behind the others. Two elderly couples with no children walked in front of us. They apparently had all of the belongings, which they were allowed to take with them, packed on their backs and walked toward the border of free China.

Chapter 31

Mr. Chiu and His Son Join Us

At about midday of the sixth day, a man approached my father speaking half in Russian and half in Chinese. Introducing himself as Mr. Chiu, he asked my father if he and his little boy could walk with us. He also asked if his son could play with us kids. Mr. Chiu said that his son was very lonely and sad. He needed somebody his age to walk with. They had been alone since leaving Kuldja.

He mentioned that they also were fleeing from communists. He and his son had walked all the way from Kuldja. His son was very sad because all of his friends had been killed by the communists in Kuldja. He said, "My wife and I and my other son were separated from this son, and we had to escape from the communists, leaving him behind. After I took my wife and my other son to safety, I went back to Kuldja for our son.

"Communists raided the home where he was hiding. They accused the husband and wife and the family of being spies and traitors against the communists. They executed the whole family and dragged their bodies out into the street so the people could see what happened to those that disobeyed and did not believe in communism.

"My son was lucky. He was able to escape by crawling out the back window and running and hiding in the field away from the house. That's why he is alive and with me today. And that is why he was not executed with the rest of his friends and their family."

After hearing his story, Father said, "Of course your son can play with our kids. We would be happy to walk with you and your son to free China."

Kim, Mr. Chiu's son, immediately came up to me and saw that I could not walk straight. Right away, he told me to stand up straight and walk. Every time I would move my left leg forward, it would collapse under my weight, and I would fall. Poor Kim tried many times to help me without success. My left leg was paralyzed and contracted and had no strength in it. If I stood up straight, my leg did not reach the ground and would dangle in the air. Subsequently, Kim gave up trying to help me. He accepted me as I was and continued to play with all of us.

We all trudged along the dirt road following the two-wheeled cart. After walking all day, we sat together away from the road to rest. We still had some of the flatbread and water that the Muslim lady had given us. Father blessed the bread and thanked God for the safe journey and our new friends. We shared the flatbread and the water with Mr. Chiu and his son. We had very little flatbread left. Father broke the remaining flatbread into eleven small pieces, enough for everybody to have one piece. Father, as usual, gave one piece to each child. We had a little piece of bread with a sip of water. Nothing was left over and nothing was wasted.

We were all so exhausted from walking the whole day, we slept through the night by the side of the road without waking up. When we woke up, more and more people were traveling on the road going east toward free China.

Mr. Chiu said to my father, "Mr. Peter, you see those people walking toward free China? They want to be free and live free. That's why my family and I ran away from communism." Some of the people were carrying their belongings on their backs. Others were pulling rickshaws loaded with their household goods. Others just rode horses. All of these people were heading toward free China and fleeing communist China.

Chapter 32

Showdown at Checkpoint Charlie

By noon of the seventh day, we encountered the main wagon train. The wagons came from different directions and merged to form a big wagon train. They all joined there as one large group going east toward free China. Each wagon was pulled by at least four to six horses.

As we pulled alongside the wagon train, all the people stared at us. It was as if they did not want us to be part of the wagon train. So we stood there on the side of the road until they passed and then tagged along, bringing up the rear of the procession. Because no one objected, we felt it was safe to join it, even though we did not have a wagon but only a two-wheeled cart pulled by two old horses.

As we continued to tag along, we noticed that more and more wagons joined us, all going in the same direction. The wagons were converging on this one central road from all directions.

Toward late afternoon of that day, the wagon train stopped. Mr. Chiu said that this must be the river where we would cross the bridge to free China.

Mr. Chiu went to the front of the wagon train. He suddenly came running back shouting, "Mr. Peter! Mr. Peter! We have a big problem!" With a frightened look on his face, he exclaimed, "The communists blew up the bridge! But we still can walk across on the planks going over the river. The planks are very narrow. Only one person can walk across at a time. It is very dangerous. The current in the river is very strong and the water is deep. What we do now, Mr. Peter?"

Father prayed silently and thought, *We are too close to freedom. We can't give up now! We have come this far under God's guidance. We must go forward at all costs. God will guide us!*

All the people in the wagon train were very confused and panicked. They did not know what to do. The people had no way to cross from communist China to free China. The communists had blown up the bridge to keep the people from escaping. Now all of them were trapped at the border and would be forced to go back to their villages and possibly face execution, prison, and labor camps. This would be their punishment for trying to escape from communism and their reward for not accepting communism as the true god.

The wagon master tried to get his six horses to pull his wagon across the river. Every time he would urge the horses into the water, they would rear up, turn around, and run in the opposite direction. The other wagons tried and also failed to get their horses to cross the river.

Father looked at the situation and said, "We cannot stay here. It is too dangerous for us to stay on this side of the river. We are so close to freedom and yet so far away. If we hesitate on this side of the river and get caught, it will mean death for me and my family.

"Therefore, we must cross the river now or die trying to reach free China. Otherwise, it is the end of our journey. We will perish here. If we get caught on this side of the river, they will have no mercy on us. They will immediately send us back to Russia, to Siberian labor camps and execution."

With his usual soft voice, he talked to the horses, encouraging them to be calm. Holding onto the horses' bridles, he led them slowly from the back of the wagon train up to the front, next to the lead wagon. Everybody watched our father and his kids walking beside the two-wheeled cart.

The wagon master shouted, "Go back. It is too dangerous! You will all be killed!"

My father acted as if he did not hear a thing. He only knew and heard what God told him to do. His mind focused on keeping his horses calm and talking to them with a soft voice as we waited for Mr. Chiu to start helping our family cross the narrow planks in the river. One by one, Mr. Chiu helped all the children, including his son, across the slender bridge to the free China side of the river.

Once all the children were safely there, Mr. Chiu helped Mother, who had an infant in her arms, walk across. Mother was very frightened but also understood that if we stayed on this side of the river we would be deported and probably killed. Once Mother and her baby were safely across, Mr. Chiu turned around and waved at my father. This was his signal to Father. Father would slowly cross the river with the cart and then would rejoin the rest of the family safely on the other side.

My father and I were the last family members left on the communist side of the river. My father would not allow me to hobble on one leg across the narrow planks. He feared that I would stumble, fall into the river, and drown. He looked up at me sitting on the cart and said, "Let us pray."

After praying, Father climbed onto the two-wheeled cart and sat next to me. Then he gently slapped the reins on the horses' backs and with his soft, pleasant voice, urged the horses into the water.

Everybody in the wagon train shouted, "It is too dangerous. Don't go! You, your crippled son, and your horses will be swept downstream by the strong raging current and drown!"

Father ignored all the commotion and acted as if he did not hear the comments that people were making. He focused on talking gently and softly to the horses and encouraging them to go across the river slowly.

People from the wagon train ran to the cart and said, "No. No. Go back! It is too dangerous. You will die!" Everybody was sure that father was taking his horses, his son, and himself to certain death. However, did they know that he would be killed by the communists if he did not try to cross the river? We overheard one man say that at least Father's wife and some of his children would survive and be safe in free China.

Father appeared to be in a trance. He did not see or hear the people who were around the cart trying to stop it and turn it around. They even tried to grab the horses' bridles in an effort to stop us from going into the turbulent current of the river. The horses only heard and responded to their master's voice. The people around the cart finally gave up and walked away.

The horses slowly waded deeper into the water toward the middle of the river. As the two-wheeled cart slowly and steadily inched its way across the violently raging river, and reached the middle of the river, the water was deeper, flowed more swiftly, and had a strong, swirling current.

We noticed that the horses' bellies touched the water, but that did not stop them. Father encouraged them to keep moving forward. He knew that if the horses stopped in the river, the wheels would instantly sink into the river's soft bottom, and they would never make it. They slowly inched their way closer and closer to the other side of the river. Here the water was calmer. It was getting shallow, and the current was not as strong.

As the cart approached the far side of the river, the horses gained solid footing in the shallow water and began to walk faster. With each step the horses took, it brought them and us closer to free China. That meant freedom for our family. Within a couple more minutes, our horses were on dry ground, on the free China side of the river!

As we neared dry ground, all the people in the wagon train shouted and threw their hats into the air. They were amazed that we had made it across the river. When they realized we had made it across with two old horses, they got their horses to go into the water and across the river. Before long, the entire wagon train had crossed the river and was safe on the free China side. Now they came and thanked my father for leading the way and for helping the wagon train to cross.

Just as the rest of the family approached the cart, three communist cars drove up to where father and I were still sitting on the cart. Each car had a small red flag attached to the antenna. These three cars were on the free China side of the river. This meant that the communists had some authority in free China as well. They had the authority to patrol both sides of the river.

A man, who had gotten out of one of the communist cars, was questioning my father. Mother kept asking Father what was going on. What was the problem?

The man asked my father if she was his wife and these were all of their children. Father replied, "Yes. This is my wife and the rest of our children."

The man said to my father, "You are a Russian. You don't belong in China. You need to go to Russia where you and your family belong. You and your family need to go to Russia where they will treat you well.

"You are truly a remarkable-looking, white Russian. You have gray hair and deep blue eyes. You are very tall and very strong and brave looking. You are of Russian heritage. You must go back to Russia where your roots are! You must go back to Russia where you will be treated according to your Russian heritage, not Chinese heritage.

"You and your family don't belong in China. You and your wife were born in Russia. Therefore, you are automatically Russian citizens regardless of where you live or you go. You must come with us now, and we will help you."

However, Father said to the Russian communist soldiers, "We have lived in China for over fifteen years. We belong here. All of us have Chinese documents. We have no Russian documents. We do not need Russian documents in China. We only need our Chinese documents that we have with us now."

The communist soldier stated that he would give us Russian documents, immediately, in exchange for our Chinese documents if we traveled back to Russia. Father said, "No. We are happy here, and we want to stay here in China. We do not wish to go back to Russia with you. Thank you for your generous offer."

While this man was talking to Father, the other three men were hurriedly taking the children and shoving them into their cars. Father repeated, "Look, I have Chinese documents. We have been living in China for over fifteen years. We belong in China. All of our documents are Chinese. We live here."

By now, they had half of the children in their cars and tried to force my mother and the baby to get in the car as well. The Chinese guards and Mr. Chiu saw what they were doing and ran over to us. They tried to stop the communists from putting all of us into their cars. The communist guards ignored the Chinese soldiers and continued to push the rest of the kids and my mother into their cars!

The Chinese guards immediately pointed their rifles at the communists and loudly yelled, "Stop! You can't do that to these people! They are in free China, and you cannot force them to go back to communist China!"

By then more and more Chinese border guards saw the commotion and came running to help. The Chinese guards realized what the communist soldiers were doing. They immediately went over and ordered all the children out of the cars.

However, the communists would not allow the children to get out of the cars. The communist soldiers took up defensive positions and stood between their vehicles and the Chinese soldiers, thus preventing the Chinese guards from approaching and taking the children out of their cars.

The commander of the Chinese border guards, hearing the commotion, ran to the front and asked what was happening? Mr. Chiu, waving his arms wildly, explained everything in a loud voice and in Chinese to the Chinese commander as he pointed at my siblings sitting in the communists' cars. The Chinese commander immediately ordered six of his border guards to point their guns directly at the communists and instructed them to shoot to kill if the communist soldiers tried to interfere! He ordered his other border guards to get the children out of the cars.

The communists did not like that. They stood their ground and did not move as the Chinese border guards slowly and cautiously walked around them to remove the children from the cars.

The communists knew that they were outnumbered, outgunned, and on the wrong side of the border to attempt any more moves. They stood motionless as the Chinese guards took all of the children and Mother a safe distance away from the dangerous situation.

The Chinese commander, looking at the communist guards, told them, in a very derogatory, demeaning, and insulting way, "Go, swine. You have no right to force these people to go back! These people are in free China. They don't have to go back if they don't want to." Then the

Chinese border commander told the communist soldiers to leave and to stop harassing people. With those words, the communists got in their cars and drove off.

Now we were all happy. The unexpected showdown was over, and God was on our side to help us win the battle. The Chinese commander of the border guard told us that we would not be bothered too much by them along the border. "You people can go where you need to go. Just remember that there are pockets of communists all over free China. They do not have as much power in this part of China and Mongolia, however, as they do in Xinjiang, China."

Chapter 33

On the Silk Road

The Marco Polo Route

Mr. Chiu, who was still with us, said that he and his son needed to go on the road that led southeast to Jiayuguan Village in Gansu Province where his wife and family were waiting for him. Mr. Chiu said that this village had been built against the Great Wall of China and that it was very safe. Part of the Great Wall surrounded the village. The only way in and out of the village was through the main gate.

However, there was a small side door just big enough for a person to walk through. This small door remained unlocked all night. Therefore, people came in and out through it if needed. This doorway was mainly used by goat herders, who came into the village after the main gate was closed. Sometimes they had a hard time rounding up their goats out in the desert. By the time they did this and reached the main gate, it was already closed. Therefore, they had to go through the small side door (THE NEEDLE GATE) to get inside the village for the night.

"Mr. Peter, you and your family come with me. It will be much safer traveling on this road for you and your family going southeast."

Father appreciated the offer, but he had a strong urge to go northeast as the people had instructed him. We parted company there. Mr. Chiu followed the road going southeast. We headed northeast on the Silk Road, trying to get as far away as possible from communist-controlled regions. The road going northeast bordered Xinjiang Province (communist China) and Gansu Province (free China). Communists were all along the border, so we had to be very careful and stay out of sight as much as possible.

Our road meandered through many tall sand dunes. Some dunes towered so high that a two-story building could hide behind one. We stayed closer to the road where the ground was more firm. Closer to the dunes, the ground was very sandy and soft. If we became stuck in the soft, deep sand, we would probably never get out.

The road followed the Chinese communist border going northeast before eventually turning east away from the border. We were in southern Mongolia, which was much safer than in communist China. However, we were told to be careful and try to travel at night. Night travel was much safer because of our proximity to the border and the fact that the communists had jurisdiction on both sides of the border. The communists had a bad habit of extending their control beyond the designated borders and would cause trouble every chance they got.

14. Photo of sand dunes

We continued walking in the desert for three weeks, Following Marco Polo's old route (The Silk Road). Water was available in the deep wells that were one day's walk apart from each other along road. There was always at least one caravan resting and getting water from a deep well for their camels and themselves.

We had no ropes or buckets to retrieve the water from the deep wells. The camel drivers realized that we needed help. They were always eager to help us get the water for our horses and us. Then they would get water for their camels and themselves. When we came to villages, we exchanged our combs for the flatbread and water that we needed.

The road slowly trailed out of the foothills and headed toward the big mountains to the left of us. We passed a village as we were leaving the foothills. Father said, "This village is too close to the border. For sure there are communists in this village, therefore, we will go around it, pick up the trail on the other side, and keep heading toward the high mountains."

Chapter 34

A Broken Wheel

We easily found the trail on the other side of the village and headed toward the high mountains, leaving the foothills behind. As Father walked in front with the horses, he noticed the horses were straining more than usual to pull the cart, which immediately alerted him that something was wrong. As the horses slowly made their way on the trail, Father went back to look at the cart and noticed that the right wheel was wobbling badly. He stopped the cart, and we unloaded it, unhitched the horses, and tied them to the cart.

Father found a big rock and placed it next to the axle of the broken wheel. Then he found a big, broken tree branch. Using the rock as a fulcrum with the tree branch under the axle, the family helped pick the axle up while Father took the broken wheel off. Once the broken wheel was off, Father motioned for the family to ease up on the branch, which let the cart come down to rest on the ground.

Father looked around and at Mother and said, "It is going to be dark soon. Let's stay here tonight. It is half a day's walk to the village from here. I will get an early start in the morning, take the wheel, and have it fixed in the village. I'll bring the wheel back and will put it back on the axle of the cart so we can continue our journey."

Early the next morning, Father got ready to take the broken wheel down to the village. He thought he could roll it down, but the wheel would not roll because it was broken. To keep it from completely falling apart, Father had to carry the large wheel on his back to the village. The wheel, made out of wood and metal, was big and heavy.

Before he put the wheel on his back and started down the mountainside to the village, we prayed together. We prayed that God would give my father a safe trip to the village and that he would find somebody who knew how to repair the broken wheel. We also prayed that the communists would not catch my father.

Father feared going back to that village. He knew he was risking his life. He knew the communists were there. That's why we went around the village instead of going through it on the way to the mountain pass. He knew if he was caught, they would kill him. However, he had no choice.

Father said, "We need the wheel repaired, otherwise we can't travel. I will continue praying, as I walk down to the village, that God will point me to a non-Communist person who is sympathetic to Christians. I pray that this person has the tools to help me repair the broken wheel." As he slowly carried the big, heavy, broken wheel on his back to the village below, he prayed.

He thought, *At least the family is safe and away from the village. If they catch me and kill me, my family will be safe. Mother is a very resourceful woman. She knows how to survive and raise the kids by herself. If it is God's will for us to live and continue on our journey, He will guide me to the right person in the village. I will go to the village and seek out this man to help me repair my broken wheel without being seen by the communists. Then, I will return to my family with the repaired wheel and we will continue on our way.*

As he approached the edge of the village, he became more nervous. He wanted to stop, turn around, and go back. He was in a daze, confused, and lost in his fearful thoughts of being caught and killed by the communists. That would leave his wife alone and stranded on a mountainside with a broken two-wheeled cart and eight children. What would the communists do with her and the children when they found them?

Father walked slowly into the village and looked for the right house to approach. He kept on praying as he walked and said to himself, *I know God will point me to the right person in the village to help me with my problem. I will find someone who has the tools to help me fix the broken wheel.*

It was about half a day's walk to the village from where we were. Carrying the heavy wheel on his shoulders, however, Father would have to take frequent rests. It would take him longer to get to the village and back.

Father was gone all day while we sat there patiently waiting for him. We didn't know whether he had had a chance to fix the wheel or had been caught by the communists, sent to prison in Russia or executed.

Mother cried and said that they probably caught him and killed him, and we would never see him again. Mother said, "Let us pray right now. Let us pray that God will protect Father from the communists and that He will give him strength to find someone to help him fix the wheel so that we can continue on our journey."

After praying, Mother continued to cry. We were all sad. We didn't know what to do. We tried to comfort mother and tell her that he would come back. But mother said, "No, he is not coming back. They caught him and killed him. We will never see Father again."

The rest of the afternoon, we sat together looking down the road toward the village, which was not visible. We had passed the village early the previous morning, so it was too far for us to see it from there.

Mother got the family together again and urged, "We must pray again for Father's safe return to us." After praying, we kept looking at the road, which wound down the mountain, hoping that we would see a small figure walking toward us. All afternoon, we thought that we saw father walking up the mountain road but were just imagining things.

Mother continued to pray that Father would return safely to the family with the repaired wheel, but we did not see Father coming up the mountain. We became more depressed. We started to believe that he had been caught and killed by the communists. We were very sad and started to cry again.

Finally, against the setting sun, we saw a small, dark figure in the distance rolling a wheel on the uphill path toward us. We knew it had to be father.

There were no other people on the trail going up the mountain pass. We had not seen a single soul all day on this road, either going up or coming down. This was a very desolate country. Nobody traveled here alone.

It had to be father. Who else would be rolling a big wheel on the steep road up the mountain in the middle of nowhere? As he came closer, we recognized him. It was Father! Mother, ecstatic that he was alive and coming back to the family, ran down the hill to greet him with tears of joy in her eyes and the baby in her arms. The older kids went to help father roll the big wheel toward the cart.

By the time Father and the kids rolled the repaired wheel close to the broken-down cart, it was too dark to do anything that night. Besides, Father was exhausted from rolling that heavy wheel up the trail. Thank God Father was alive and safely with us. We were all thrilled to see Father again. We had been praying all day that he would be safe and would return to us.

Relating the events of the day, Father explained, "There was a man in the village who knew about working with wagons and how to repair them. He had tools in his small, one-room blacksmith shop to help me fix the wheel, but he did not know how to use them. Since I had experience repairing wheels on the farm, I showed him how to use his tools. Both of us working together were able to repair the broken wheel. He also gave me the axle grease that we needed to make the wheels work better, roll easier, and keep from breaking."

Father added, "I gave him two of our combs. He said his family needed a comb and that his wife and three daughters all have long, black hair, and they have nothing to comb them out with. So the combs will help him and his family." He also gave father some food and water to take with him. The man was very happy that he was able to help father fix the wheel.

The next morning, the family was up at the crack of dawn. As before, we put the old tree trunk under the axle and over the rock, using it as a fulcrum. Mother and the older kids got on the far end of the tree trunk and pushed down on it causing the other end of the tree trunk with the cart axle on it to go up and raise the cart and the axle in the air.

In the meantime, Father and Tony repositioned the repaired wheel on the axle. Once they got the wheel on the axle, they secured it and asked the family to lower the axle until the wheel was touching the ground.

Now the wheel was repaired and back on the cart's axle. It was secured and ready to roll again. It didn't take long for the two older boys to hitch the horses to the cart. Once this was done, we stood together in a circle, took our hats off, and prayed, thanking God that the wheel was repaired and the family was together again. Now we were ready to continue our journey.

Chapter 35

Up the Mountain

As we slowly ascended the winding road, it became very narrow, rocky, and steep. We could not keep up the easy pace that we had before but had to take frequent rests. The horses also got tired very quickly and needed to rest.

As the road continued to wind upward even more steeply, we had to place rocks behind the wheels to keep the cart from rolling backward down the mountain and into the deep ravines. It was too much of a burden for the horses to keep the cart from rolling back. Initially, we only stopped occasionally to place rocks behind the wheels. Then we had to do it more frequently. After we secured the cart with the wedged rocks, the horses would rest, and we would rest at the same time.

We continued our upward struggle on this treacherous road. Now it became so steep that we had to push the cart to help the horses move forward. It became more difficult for the horses and for us. We had to stop every few feet to put rocks in place behind the wheels. If the cart ever started rolling back, it would gain momentum, and we would not be strong enough to stop it. Most likely, it would drag the horses off the cliff to their death hundreds of feet below in the deep gorge.

15. Photo of the type of terrain we encountered

On the third day of our journey on this treacherous, winding path to the high mountains, we encountered a very narrow spot in the road. Father knew that the cart was too wide to get through. The horses could make it across, but as the wheels of the cart approached that spot, only one wheel would be on solid ground against the mountainside. The other wheel would be on the soft, slanted, washed-out part of the edge of the road. Father knew that if the wheel hit that soft spot, it would slide sideways and drag the cart and the horses off the road. They would fall down to their deaths in the deep gorge hundreds of feet below.

Father gave Tony and Benny one stick apiece and said, "Use these sticks to dig all the soft dirt away from the road until the bottom of the hole is hard and very rocky. When you hit solid rock, you can stop digging. I will roll some big rocks from across the road to fill the hole that you dig so it will be solid enough for the wheel to go across without danger."

It worked just as Father said. After the boys dug the hole per Father's instructions, we helped Father carry two or three big rocks to fill the hole. Now the edge was solid and a little higher than the rest of the road. Father said, "Now the road is wide enough for the cart to go through."

He helped mother out of the cart and told her to walk behind the cart where it was safe. Then he went to the front of the cart and guided the horses very slowly and carefully across the narrow area. While Father guided the horses up front, all the kids were pushing the cart from the back to make sure that it would not become stuck in the bad spot but would continue to move slowly, smoothly, and steadily across the homemade patch job.

Slowly and very carefully, we pushed the cart across that dangerously narrow spot. The wheel went over the repaired place without any problems. Now we continued inching our way up the mountain. There were many rocks on the path, both big and small, which blocked our way in places, making it very difficult for the horses. Father and the older two boys, Tony and Benny, moved the rocks off the narrow road. They had to do this frequently throughout the day.

We noticed that there were places where the trail widened for a short distance before again becoming very narrow and dangerous. The narrow, steep path winding around the mountain reminded us of a huge snake that had wrapped itself around a giant, trying to squeeze the last breath of life out of him.

As we slowly approached a wide spot in the road, Father proclaimed, "It is getting dark, and all of us are tired and in need of a rest. This is a good place for us to spend the night. It is wide enough for us to unhitch the horses and walk around the cart freely." Tony and Benny unhitched them and tied them to the cart. Then all of us huddled together on the ground against the mountainside to keep warm and away from the steep drop-off on the other side.

As always, the family was up early the next day. Tony and Benny hitched the horses to the cart, and after praying, we continued on our way. The horses were rested and seemed to pull the cart with much more ease. We did not have to push the cart as we had before this. We still had to frequently let the horses rest by wedging rocks behind the wheels.

By midday, we found ourselves still ascending the steep trail. We noticed it was getting much colder as we neared the higher elevation in the mountains. Everybody was exhausted after walking most of the morning and pushing the cart at times.

As we neared a wider area, we were very tired and thought this would be a good place to stop and rest. As the horses stopped, Tony and Benny placed big rocks behind the cart's wheels. Once it had been secured, Father, Tony, and Benny attended to the horses. In the meantime, Mother spread a blanket on the ground behind the cart where the other kids sat down to rest.

Everyone rested except for Alex. He was still full of energy. He was like a little mountain goat. He decided to climb the steep, rocky mountain directly above where mother and the other children were sitting on the blanket.

Suddenly, Alex screamed, and all of us on the blanket looked up to see what was wrong. We instantly knew what the problem was: A big boulder was crashing down the very steep mountainside. As it came careening down, it picked up speed. The gigantic rock was headed straight for the family and the cart! Now we knew why Alex screamed.

Everything was happening so fast that we didn't have time to move or to duck. All of us were petrified as we watched the massive bolder heading straight for us. The boulder was big enough to crush all of us, along with the horses and the cart. We closed our eyes and prayed because that's all we had time to do.

We heard a big thud, the ground shook, and it was over. A solid cliff wall was next to us. It protruded straight upward above us. The giant boulder hurling downward apparently hit this sheer rocky mountain wall with enough force that it was propelled over us. The boulder flew over the group and plunged straight into the river gorge hundreds of feet below.

Father and the boys came running from the front to ensure that we were okay. We were somewhat shaken but otherwise okay. Father immediately got us into a tight group, and we prayed, thanking God for safety in this incident and that nobody was hurt.

By now, Alex was scrambling down from his mountainous adventure, crying as he came. He got a sympathy hug from Mother. He exclaimed, "I didn't know the big boulder was loose. When I stepped on it, it started moving, and I screamed because I was afraid it would hurt somebody!"

Father scolded Alex for climbing above the group and almost causing a disaster. Thank God that although everybody was shook up a little, nobody was hurt.

The next morning everybody was up early because it was too cold to sleep. We got the horses and the cart ready. After a short prayer thanking God for our safe journey thus far, we felt energized and ready to go forward. We began slowly pushing the cart up the steeply winding, treacherous road toward what appeared to be the top of the mountains.

We slowly came around the bend expecting the road to level off and to start our steep descent. To our surprise, the big mountains on either side of us retained their majestic beauty and height, thus fading into the distant horizon on either side of the road, leaving a beautiful flat panoramic view directly in front of us as far as the eye could see!

The road became wider and had no more dangerous, steep gorges for us to worry about. The family, instead of pushing the cart, was trying to keep up with the cart. The downhill slope made it easier for the horses to pull the cart.

Now we faced new challenges—the cold desert wind and sand blowing directly into our faces. We struggled to see through this vast sand veil blowing across the horizon. We saw a wasteland with massive protruding sand dunes everywhere and the occasional low hill here and there.

As we struggled against these natural, winter, desert elements, we were getting very cold. This encouraged us to seek any shelter that we could find. Everybody was freezing, so we all started looking for shelter. Far off in the distance among the sand dunes and through the blowing sand, we could make out a tiny black building with what appeared to be camels in front of it. However, it was too far to tell if they were camels or other types of beasts of burden. This building was our destination.

Chapter 36

Oasis in the Gobi

As we approached this low building constructed with straw, mud bricks, and logs, it did not resemble a restaurant. Outside the building were many camels, which were loaded with various boxes, sacks, and bundles. Many caravans that were traveling had stopped there to eat, sleep, and rest their camels. This was an oasis for them. The numerous camels told us there were many travelers inside the building.

We walked in and found a dark corner away from the big crowd. We huddled on rough wooden benches around a low makeshift table constructed of rough boards. We were frightened. We sat crowded together, looking like a cluster of mushrooms coming out of a compost pile or a dirty pile of old clothes that somebody had dumped in the corner. Our ragged clothes were covered with dirt and dust. No facial features were clearly visible except for the whites of our eyes.

It was nice and cozy inside. We quickly warmed up inside the building and started to relax. The aroma of food permeated the air. It was so strong that we felt if we could only take a deep enough breath of this powerful scent it would satisfy the deep hunger that we felt inside our starving, malnourished bodies.

As we sat there, Father suggested we pray that God would help us. After the prayer he said, "Tava and Tony, you two go back to the kitchen in the restaurant and ask for the noodle water. They boil the noodles two or three times in the same water. After boiling the third bunch of noodles in the same water, the water becomes very soupy. They throw this soupy water away and get fresh water. This discarded, soupy, noodle water is very nutritious. It will help us to survive several days more."

Soon after Tava and Tony left for the kitchen, Father noticed Tony coming back with a man following him. The man was dressed like a cook. He said something to Tony, who pointed to the table where we were sitting. The man looked at us, saw all of the children, turned around, and went back in the kitchen. Shortly after that, Tava and Tony brought two pots of hot noodle water to the table. The cook came out of the kitchen with nine wooden bowls and nine large wooden spoons to help us eat this soupy water.

At the same time, a well-dressed man with a servant approached the table where we were sitting and said that he saw us come in and sit in the corner. "I looked at you and the children, and I realized that you and your family needed some food and rest. We purchased more bread then we need. You can have it for your children and for yourself. We have more than enough for us.

"I paid for one room with meals, for two nights, for two people, but my business urgently demands that my servant and I leave today. My room is paid for another night. I want you and your family to use that room tonight. Stay there and get rested up.

"My mother lives not very far from here. She would love to have you and your family stay with her. You and your family can rest there for one or two weeks. Then you and your family can continue on your journey!"

Immediately my father said, "Thank you so much for your hospitality and for offering your mother's house to us, but we cannot stay longer than tonight. We must continue on our journey." It was as if an invisible force was urging him not to hesitate but to go quickly forward.

After eating the flatbread and drinking the noodle water in the restaurant, we were all full. Father thanked God for the wonderful people in the restaurant who helped us get food. He also thanked God for the gentleman who gave us the flatbread and a warm room to spend the night in so we could rest before continuing our journey.

Father, Tony, and Benny unhitched the horses from the cart. They fed the horses and made sure that they had plenty of water for the night.

While they were doing this, Mother found the combs that Father made for the trip. She took some and, going back into the restaurant, sold the combs for some food for our trip. Mother was able to get a bag of corn for the horses and a bag of cornmeal and wheat flour for us. Father looked at that cornmeal and wheat flour and said "Yes. We will need this on the road."

We had a very warm, restful night of sleep for the first time in many months. The room had only one bed, so everybody slept on the floor except for Father, Mother, and the baby. We were all up at dawn, ready to continue our journey. Father, with the two older boys, had gotten up earlier to feed and water the horses. They hitched the horses to the cart, and we put all of our belongings back in, prayed, and continued on our journey to an unknown destination in a strange land.

After walking some distance away from the restaurant, Father stopped the cart and said we must pray again and thank God for the restful night that we had had. We needed to pray especially for the gentleman that had given us a warm room to rest in for the night and for the food that he had given us. We should also pray that God would watch over him and protect him as he traveled to his destination. Indeed, he had been a man sent by God to help us on our journey. Then we would pray that God's will would be done wherever He led us.

During the time Tava and Tony were in the kitchen of the restaurant, I sat next to Mother. I felt confused, somewhat bewildered, and scared by all the unfamiliar people in the building. I nestled closer to my mother as I felt the heat from her body and the baby, Nikki, moving in her lap. I felt very warm and secure sitting next to her among all of the strange people around us in the smoke-filled room.

As I looked around, I was intrigued with all the people. They had strange clothes and hats. Some had furry hats. Others had white cloths wrapped around their heads like turbans. Others had no hats or head coverings. Many had only skullcaps on their heads! All were unique. All of them had their own favorite place in the restaurant. Some stood or leaned against the wall, some sat around crude wooden tables made out of rough boards, and some stood around in groups, smoking and talking to their fellow travelers.

In one corner, a group of men sat on the floor, passionately discussing their issues as they puffed subconsciously on their long pipes, which produced columns of bluish smoke. As the smoke left their pipes, it swirled lazily, spiraling up toward the ceiling. There it intermingled with all the other columns of smoke to produce a thick, dense, grayish-blue haze. This haze hovered above the people in the room. Through this dense cloudlike haze, it was difficult to distinguish a person's features.

All of the people appeared to be content in this smoked-filled room. With passion and intensity, they carefully listened to the comments of their comrades, eagerly answering their questions. They ignored the smoke-filled room and the haze as they continued to engage each other deeper in their relentlessly intriguing conversations about travels to strange foreign countries on the other side of the Gobi Desert.

All the people in the restaurant were travelers and merchants from different countries. They were all dressed differently, in their native attire. However, everybody was covered with the same desert dust that settled on their clothes, faces, and hands, as they traveled the Gobi Desert. After eating and resting, they would continue on the road across the Gobi toward their respective destinations.

This restaurant was one of many oases on the Silk Road in the Gobi Desert. From these oases in the desert, the Silk Road divided into many branches where the travelers and the merchants would carry their spices, herbs, and silk to foreign lands, such as Greece, Turkey, Rome, and the rest of the known world.

All of these people smoked different types of pipes. Some smoked short pipes and others smoked long pipes. Cigars and cigarettes were smoked by those who could afford them. Some of the people even rolled their own cigarettes—the homemade kind.

They had no tobacco and no money to buy any, so they used dried animal manure instead of tobacco. Dried animal manure was cheap, free, and readily available everywhere there were animals. When the animal deposited the manure on the ground, it was fresh, smelly, soupy, or firm. It was carefully picked up and dried and then was ready for use.

In the desert, fuel such as wood or coal was very scarce. Animal manure was nothing more than digested or partially digested grass. It also was dried and used as a source of fuel in the homes. In small amounts, it was rolled up in a piece of paper and smoked as a cigarette. Paper was a very pricy commodity that everybody desired, but not everybody had!

Horse trading and bartering were always going on among the travelers. At the end of all the trading and bartering, everybody always got what he had bargained for and was content with his transactions. After an evening of horse trading, bargaining, and exchanging tales of their journeys across the Gobi, they retired to their respective rooms and tents to rest and to get ready for a long journey across the Gobi toward their distant destinations in the far countries of the world.

Chapter 37

A Strange Village

We were traveling eastward in the remote part of the southern region of the Gobi Desert. Mother had Nikki in her arms and sat on top of the cart pulled by our two old horses. Father was up front leading the horses. The rest of the seven kids followed behind the cart in a tight group. It was getting late in the day and after traveling all day, we were tired and walking very slowly.

I always tried to walk by placing my left hand on my left leg, which was the one that was paralyzed. I tried to walk in a half-upright position. This was slow and difficult. I could not keep this up all the time.

Blisters had formed on my left hand and knee. These blisters broke and were very painful. When the blisters broke, they would secrete clear fluid, which later turned into bloodied fluid as I continued to press my knee with my hand in order to walk. I could not keep going like this. When I became exhausted, I would get on the ground on my one good leg supported by my hands and move like a dog.

This was faster and easier for me than walking. I didn't have to endure all the pain in my knee and didn't get blisters. I did not have to depend on Tava or Tony to carry me as much. When I would get to the point where I couldn't move anymore, even in this position, I would sit on the ground, rest, and watch my family slowly walk farther and farther away from me. If Tava or Tony glanced back and saw me sitting down, she or he would quickly run back, pick me up, carry me to the cart, and place me next to mother. Tava usually was the one who came to my rescue when I became exhausted and unable to move anymore.

Suddenly, Father said, "Look, look, out there in the distance. There is a small village ahead of us." As we approached the settlement, people came running toward us from every direction. We were afraid. We immediately and instinctively closed ranks. We walked very close together and held hands as we followed closely behind the two-wheeled cart.

Tava, for fear of losing me, picked me up and carried me on her back as we walked through the small village. The villagers mobbed us. With inquisitive, bewildered expressions on their faces, they peered at our strange features.

We were afraid of them. They seemed very strange to us, with their straight black hair, different facial features, and strange, unfamiliar language. Father, who was tall with light brown hair, blue eyes, and white skin, was about a foot taller than anybody else in the village, as far as we could see.

The entire crowd was looking at us. We were a fairly dirty and unique looking group—six kids walking behind a two-wheeled cart with the oldest child carrying her crippled little brother on her back. My mother, who was covered with dust like the rest of us, was sitting on top of the cart clutching her eight-month-old infant tightly. She was very scared, thinking that someone was going to snatch her baby right out of her arms.

As we continued walking toward the center of the village, the crowd around us grew. We became more frightened. Father stopped the cart and motioned for the kids to come to the front of the cart. He positioned Tava with me on her back next to the horse. Father stood on the other side of Tava. All the smaller children were behind Tava and Father, with Tony and Benny bringing up the rear. That way all the children were within eyesight of Mother, Tony, Benny, Tava, and Father.

We slowly started walking again, and the crowd continued to get bigger. They kept coming closer and closer until we could feel their breath on our faces. As they leaned into our faces, their breath was malodorous and raunchy. They kept looking at our eyes—our eyes were not slanted like theirs. Our hair was not black and thick. Our skin was much lighter than theirs was. They pointed at Father's height, his brown hair, and his deep blue eyes.

We could not tell at this point whether we were more afraid of them or they were more afraid of us. We spoke Russian and some Arabic but could not understand their language, and they could not understand us.

Father, with a smile on his face, slowly continued walking. Calm and collected, he would smile, nod his head in agreement, and keep on going. From time to time, he looked back to make sure all of the kids were with him. Mother was sitting on the cart clinging tightly to the infant in her arms and looking very frightened. She was overwhelmed by the murmuring in a language she did not understand. To her, it looked like the large mob was ready to kill us.

As we passed the center of the village, Father said, "Let's go faster and get out of this village. We are not safe here. We will not stop in this village as we planned. These people do not look very friendly. We must get out of the village as quickly as we can."

Once we neared the other side of town, the crowd thinned out, and we continued out of the village and into the vast open desert before us. As we left the village behind us, we felt more at ease and were not as frightened. Peace and quiet were what we needed to settle our nerves. We pressed forward at quicker pace without even looking back.

We walked the rest of the day, trying to put as much distance as possible between us and the village before dark. As the darkness crept over the countryside like a black cloud, Father said, "Now that we're in the middle of nowhere, far away from the village and especially from the strange people, we must stop, pray, and rest here! We must rest our horses here as well."

We sat on the ground in a circle. Father started a small fire with some pieces of coal that we had. When the fire was hot, Mother boiled some water, put cornmeal and flour in it, and made a paste out of it. As soon as Mother finished boiling the flour and the cornmeal, Father immediately extinguished the fire with sand. As soon as the coal pieces were cool, we placed them back on the cart to take with us so we could use them again.

With the fire out, it was much darker since our eyes had not yet adjusted to the darkness. We started grumbling, but Father said, "It is darker but much safer for us. So let's settle down, get a few hours of rest, and then we can keep on going."

We were starving. In the darkness, we still could see the pot of boiled cornmeal. All of us kids had our eyes glued on the small pot. We were all waiting for it to cool off so we could eat it. It looked like paste but smelled so good that we wanted to eat it right away, sand and all. As we sat there, Tony was apparently very hungry. He eyed the boiled cornmeal more than any of us kids. He quickly reached over into the pot, grabbed a handful of this paste, and started to stuff it into his mouth. Father instantly grabbed a big wooden spoon and hit Tony on the forehead, breaking the wooden spoon into two pieces!

The surprised, stunned expression on Tony's face—his mouth open with food dripping out of his mouth—was priceless to see. We all felt sorry for Tony. He started to cry, and all of us wanted to cry with him.

Father said, "We must give thanks to God for the safety of our trip thus far and especially for this meal that He provided for us." He added, "Even the Muslims pray before they eat." Father continued by saying that we must always be thankful to God for everything that we had, most of all, the food and the safety of the trip. We stopped whatever we were doing, took off our hats and caps, and Father prayed. He thanked God for the safety of the journey and for the food that God had provided that night. He concluded by saying, "May His will be done in all the things that we do. Amen."

After each one of us ate a tiny portion of the boiled cornmeal paste portioned out by father, he took the remainder of the paste and made a big ball out of it, which was almost the size of a soccer ball. He carefully squashed it together, wrapped it in a cloth, and told us that it was going to be our food for as long as it lasted. All of us looked at the big ball of paste and asked, "Are we going to eat that, with all that sand and dirt in it?" Father, without saying a word, rewrapped the ball of paste with a cloth and placed it on the cart.

We rested for several hours and with the moon shining bright during the night, started walking again. After walking another night, we were very hungry. Now, that paste of cornmeal and flour was very appealing, dirt and all! We were so hungry that we were willing to devour it.

He unwrapped the ball of paste and pinched off a small amount to put into each child's mouth. He would take a small portion for his wife and himself in the same manner. Then he would rewrap the ball in the sandy cloth and put it back in the cart. Nothing was wasted. This ball of paste with sand and dirt was our source of survival for as long as it lasted.

We traveled for weeks toward the rising sun after leaving the oasis. The countryside was sandier and very dry. We could see very little vegetation on the horizon. Basically, what we saw were low bushes here and there and lots of sand. There were no trees.

Father and Mother were very careful with the small amount of food and water that we ate. We had cherished and had eaten sparingly the flatbread, which the man had given to us at the restaurant, until it had been gone. Now all we had left was some water and the sandy ball of paste wrapped in a dirty cloth. Father said we would share it as long as it lasted. Maybe by then, God would provide more food for us.

Father thought the news of us being in that strange village would spread very rapidly, and the bad people would know that we were walking in this direction. He said we must continue walking quickly to get as far away as we could from this part of the country to keep ahead of all the fighting.

Father prayed again, asking for God's guidance in making the right decisions. After resting, we started walking again. Walking at night was better because the moon was very bright and made it very easy to follow Father, who walked briskly as if he knew exactly where he was going. We followed him quietly across the desert night, just like a bunch of scared baby rats sneaking in the shadows of darkness, trailing their mother, trying their best not to be spotted and devoured by predators that lurked in the shadows of the desert night.

After walking most of the night, we would be very hungry and tired. Father knew we needed a rest. By early morning, he would find a secluded spot away from the main road and behind some low area or rocks that were big enough to hide the cart, the horses, and the family. The rocks would be some distance from the road, which made it safer for us and more difficult for someone to find us. As I said previously, there were no trees in the area. We would go behind tall sand dunes, unhitch the horses, and lie down on the ground and rest.

One night we ran out of food completely. Oh, I should not say completely. We still had that ball of gluey, boiled cornmeal and flour that Father had wrapped in the old piece of cloth and had put in the cart for the future. We had eaten no food all night and were starving.

Father went to the cart and brought back the ball of cornmeal and flour paste. It had been in the cart for several days. Each day, the ball had shrunk. Now it was much smaller and was full of sand and dirt along with the boiled cornmeal and flour. It sounded horrible, but at this point in time, we were starving and didn't care. We were willing to eat anything that resembled food. Father brushed the dirt off the cloth, unwrapped the ball, and put a small pinch of paste in each child's mouth. Then he took some for Mother and himself.

Many times Father, instead of resting, would go looking for water or some type of food for the family. Sometimes he would be gone two to three hours or sometimes half a day but would always bring something back. He always provided for the family and the horses.

Chapter 38

Catholic Missionary

We continued our journey in the Gobi Desert on the Silk Road for several weeks, trying to keep a low profile during the day and walking at night. It was during this time that my older sister, Lydia, got very sick to the point where she could not walk. Father placed her next to Mother on the two-wheeled cart.

As we forged ahead on our journey into the desert, we came across another small village. We stopped there, and a man, who spoke some Russian, came out. Father found out that he was a Catholic missionary working with the Chinese and the Mongolian people in that area. The missionary took one look at Lydia and said, "She must be brought into the house and cared for. She has smallpox."

He left the one-room shack and shortly returned with a big apple, which he divided for the kids. Because Lydia was sick, she got the biggest piece. After eating the delicious, fresh apple, we all felt better physically, mentally, and spiritually. Even Lydia, as sick as she was, managed to work up a smile on her red, swollen face, which was covered with sores.

The missionary kept giving Lydia medicine, and after ten days, she started to feel and act better. Her fever broke and her temperature dropped slowly. We noticed that the sores were drying up on her face, and there were not any new sores on her face or body. Lydia became more cheerful, pleasant, and started to smile.

As Lydia continued to improve, Father became more anxious and wanted to leave. He insisted that we must go. He kept telling the missionary it was urgent that we continue to travel. We could not stop there. This was not the end of our journey. We had to go on!

"But where are you going?" the missionary asked. "You have eight children and a wife, a two-wheeled cart and two old horses. One of your horses is very sick. Look at all that pus draining out of the large open abscess on his neck. How far can you get under these conditions?

"This is the Gobi Desert, one of worst wastelands of the world. People with camels, food, and water have died out here in the Gobi. Without proper provisions, people vanish overnight in the Gobi Desert. People travel on camels in this desert, not on old, sick horses pulling a homemade cart with eight small children walking behind it. What are you thinking, trying to go across the Gobi Desert under these circumstances? Under your conditions, my friend, you are on a journey of death. Is that your destination? Death!"

Father replied, "God knows. He wants us to continue our journey." The missionary threw up his hands in disbelief, turned around, and walked away.

FOOT NOTE :

1) SAHARA DESERT WORST DESERT IN THE WORLD
2) GOBI DESERTNNORTH WEST CHINA 2ND WORST DESERT IN THE WORLD
3) FOLLOWED BY MOJAVE DESERT IN CALIFORNIA AS THE 3RD WORST DESERT IN THE WORLD.

Even before Lydia was well, Father was getting very anxious. He said, "We must go. We must go now." When the missionary realized that Father was very adamant about going on, he knew that he could not change his mind. He saw the serious look on his face and could not argue with him.

Then the missionary said, "You must travel in that direction, going east. God will help you." He pointed to the east and said, "Go that way deeper into the Gobi Desert. There is less danger there from the communists. The communists have not penetrated that area yet. However, there are worse dangers in the Gobi Desert than the communists—robbers, wild animals, and the natural deadly elements of the desert. You will have to protect yourself and your family from all these elements of the desert. Go in peace, and may God bless you and guide you on your journey that He set before you.

"You will be safer traveling in that direction. There is a missionary working there. This missionary is another servant of God who knows the desert and knows the people who live in the desert. He lived there among those people for many years, and he ministers to them. Also, he knows medicine—everybody goes to him when they're sick. Everybody in the Gobi knows him and his good works and how he helps all the desert people in the Gobi.

"He is called 'The Holy Man' of the desert. He will help you and guide you on your journey to your destination. I will give you a letter of introduction from me to him. He knows me. I've had the opportunity to work together with him many times. You will take this letter and give it to him and he will help you. His name is George Hunter."

Father was immediately excited because he recognized the name. George Hunter was the Scottish missionary who had come and had worked among the Russian people in Kuldja (Gulja), in Xinjiang Province (Sinkiang Province), in China about ten years before we had arrived there from Russia. He had been the one who had been imprisoned in Urumqi by the communists and the Muslims for preaching about God.

Father knew about this missionary. Father took the letter and graciously thanked the missionary for all of his help: for treating Lydia with medicine, for giving us food and shelter, and for helping us recuperate and regain our strength from the journey.

Again, the missionary pointed east and said, "Go that way and you'll find this man of God who will help you. Always keep the mountains in sight. The ground is more firm and not as sandy there. Your horses will be able to pull your cart much easier there than through the sandy soil where the sand dunes are. Only men with camels survive there."

Father obviously knew the dangers of traveling through the communist territory, especially since he was a marked man. He knew that the whole purpose was to stay clear of the communists and to get away from them as far and as quickly as possible. He had escaped their snares many times in Siberia, Russia, and in Kuldja, China.

So when the missionary said to go in the direction of the Gobi Desert because the danger from it was less than that from the communists, Father knew exactly what the missionary was talking about. He knew that going east into the Gobi Desert was very dangerous, but that it was much safer than facing certain imprisonment, torture, and immediate execution if caught by the communists.

After praying with the missionary and thanking him for everything, we continued our journey. For the next several days, we journeyed east, always keeping the mountains close to us and staying on the firmer ground, thus preventing our two-wheeled cart from getting bogged down in the deep soft sand.

Chapter 39

Looking for the Holy
Man in the Desert

Traveling through the desert was very tiring. We would all push the cart to keep the horses and the cart moving. When everybody was exhausted from pushing the cart, we would stop and rest. We encountered many caravans traveling in both directions on the same trail. All the caravans were camel caravans. We did not see any horses in the caravans. We moved slowly—we would push the cart for a short distance and have to stop and rest. We kept this up for several days.

One day we came to a well in the desert. We were very thirsty and hungry but had a problem. The well was quite deep, and we had no way of getting the water out. As we stood around the well trying to figure out how we were going to get water, a camel driver came to help us. Camel drivers were always prepared for traveling in the desert. They carried buckets with long ropes attached to them. They would lower their buckets into the deep well, fill them with water, and then pull them to the surface.

Another camel driver approached the well with his bucket and rope. He also wanted to help us. Both camel drivers got water from the well. They gave water to our horses first. When the horses had enough water, they gave some water to us. After we had enough water to drink, the camel drivers gave some water to their camels to drink. Then they drank some water themselves. After everybody had enough water to drink, one of the camel drivers, who understood some Russian and Arabic, questioned us. "Where are you going?" he asked my father.

"We're looking for the holy man in the desert called George Hunter."

"Yes, we have heard of the holy man who lives in the desert. Go in that direction and you'll soon meet him. The way you travel with your horses, it may take you five days to get to his village. Stay away from the deep sand and closer to the mountains. The ground is more firm there, and you will make good time with your horses."

The camel driver continued, "This is one of the main trade routes across the Gobi Desert. It is called the Silk Road. Many camel caravans travel here. These travelers are good merchants and are well prepared to travel across the Gobi Desert. If you have trouble in the desert, they will be there to help you. To survive the desert, people must depend on each other. You must sell your horses and get camels, otherwise you will all perish in the Gobi Desert, along with your horses."

As we continued walking in the right direction, Tava began to complain of pain in her jaw. By the end of the day, she was in severe pain. We rested very little during the night. We wanted to reach the village where George Hunter was. By late afternoon of the fifth day, we spotted a village in the distance. My father said it had to be the village where Mr. Hunter lived.

My father was very concerned about Tava. Her face was extremely swollen and red. She was slurring her speech, and it was difficult to understand her. She did not look like herself anymore. She looked like she was very sleepy all the time and could not hold her head up. Her head was bobbing from side to side like a doll's head with no life. Father prayed that Mr. Hunter would have the right medicine for Tava.

As we approached the village, Mr. Hunter was walking toward us. He explained, "I have been expecting you. The camel drivers from the caravans informed me that you were on the way here. They said, 'There is a family with eight children walking toward your village looking for you. They have two small horses pulling a two-wheeled cart. One woman is riding on the cart with a baby in her arms. The rest of the children are walking behind the cart. One of the children is crippled, but he also is hobbling along behind the cart. The man is in front, leading the horses. They are walking very slowly toward your village, five day's journey back.' For the past two days I have been looking west toward the Silk Road for you. And now you and your family are here."

When we got to his house, Father immediately showed the letter of introduction from the Catholic missionary to George Hunter. Mr. Hunter read the letter and replied, "Yes, I will help you as much as I can. But first you must come inside, eat, and rest. Then we will talk."

My father asked, "Mr. Hunter, do you have any medicine? My daughter is very sick and needs help right away. Do you have any medicine to help her?"

Mr. Hunter took a closer look at Tava. He looked at her red, swollen face, felt her neck and jaw, and answered, "Yes, I can try to help her. She has an abscessed tooth." He continued to carefully observe this semi-comatose, poorly-responsive child sitting next to her mother on the cart. She was too weak to hold her head up.

After checking Tava very carefully the second time, Mr. Hunter realized that the infection had already spread around her right jaw and eye and was moving across her entire forehead. He said that the right side of her face was infected, inflamed, and very hot to the touch. She was in danger of dying very quickly unless he operated soon.

His friendly, happy face quickly changed to a very serious, concerned face. "I must do surgery on her right away. She has a severe abscessed tooth, and the infection is spreading very rapidly throughout her body. The infection is very close to her brain, and it will kill her very quickly if I do not operate on her now. Surgery must be done now, or she will die. The abscessed tooth has to be pulled, and the abscess has to be drained immediately to stop the infection from spreading and killing her. But first," he said in a quiet, gentle voice, "I will give her some medicine to keep the infection from spreading throughout the rest of her body."

After giving Tava the medicine, he prepared a mask and placed it over her face. She immediately fell asleep. While she was sleeping, he pulled her abscessed tooth and cleaned out the abscess. When she woke up, he gave her more medicine, and she fell back to sleep.

The next day, Tava was feeling much better. The swelling and redness in her face had diminished. She was slurring her speech much less when she spoke and was able to hold her head straight without wobbling or bobbing it from side to side. Now there was life in her face. She did not smile but was alive. Her voice was very weak. She still looked very weak and puny, like you could knock her over with a feather.

After about one week's rest, Tava was feeling almost like herself again. Father, as usual, was very anxious to keep moving now that Tava was feeling much better. He insisted on going as quickly as possible. Mr. Hunter kept telling my father to stay and let Tava recover from her infection, but Father had made up his mind to go and would not hear of it. He was ready to travel.

"Your family needs to rest as well," urged Mr. Hunter.

But Father insisted on going, "We must continue on our journey. We cannot delay."

Mr. Hunter asked, "If you must go now, would you consider leaving your oldest son with me to do God's work? I am getting up in years, and I need him to help me to continue to do God's work here."

Father could not agree to that. He answered, "I cannot leave my son here. I know that you badly need a worker to help you. But Tony is only a child. He still needs his parents to help him grow and mature physically and spiritually. I am sure that God will send you a helper very soon. We need to continue and finish our journey! Only He knows the end of our journey. And only He can and will tell us when our journey is at an end."

Then Mr. Hunter told us to go to Lanchow, China, and gave Father a letter of introduction to the missionaries in Lanzhou (Lanchow). You will find Mr. and Mrs. Schoerner and their family there. They are missionaries from America. They are from Moody Bible Institute in Chicago. They have missionary friends in Shanghai. They will help you more in Lanzhou (Lanchow), China."

Mr. Hunter approached Father a second time about leaving Tony with him to do missionary work there in China. He said he really needed

Tony to help him. Again, Father could not agree to that arrangement. He said, "Tony is part of our family and we cannot leave him here."

"You should follow the branch of the Silk Road going across the southern Gobi desert toward Lanzhou (Lanchow), China. In Lanzhou (Lanchow), China, the American missionaries will help you more than I can. Take this letter of introduction for Mr. and Mrs. Schoerner, who will be able to help you much more than I can from here. I understand your great burden of urgency of wanting to continue on your journey. I will do my best to help you."

About a month after Mr. Hunter pulled Tava's abscessed tooth and saved her life, Mr. Hunter died. We received the news of his death years later. We think that we were the last westerners to see George Hunter alive before he went to be with the Lord on December 20, 1946. If it were not for Mr. Hunter's accurate directions to Lanzhou (Lanchow) and the letter that he wrote to the Schoerners, we would have been lost and dead somewhere in the vast wilderness of the Gobi Desert!

Chapter 40

The Journey by the Great Wall

After placing all of our belongings on the two-wheeled cart, we prayed with Mr. Hunter and got ready to walk. Mr. Hunter said, "You must walk from here south for about twenty to twenty five days. There you will encounter the Great Wall of China. It is in sections. Over the years, it started to fall apart in some places. In other places, it is solid and extends as far as your eye can see in both directions.

"You must follow the wall going south. The wall will turn and go west. You must go through the break in the wall and continue going south along the wall. Then you will meet many travelers coming and going. Follow the wall south through the break in the wall for about ten days walking distance. Then you will encounter a large walled village, Jiayuquan Village, which was built against the Great Wall of China.

"The only way into the village will be through the main gates, which are open only during daylight hours. There is always the small gate (needle gate) that is open all night, but your cart and horses will not squeeze through this tiny gate, therefore, you have to wait outside the gate until the next morning when the main gates open at sunrise."

As we slowly walked along the wall, we met more people coming and going. Some of them were in groups. Apparently, they were from different villages and wanted to keep to themselves as they walked. The people carried sacks of clothes, chairs, and other household items that they had brought with them. Camels pulled many overloaded wagons on the road. We saw camel caravans loaded with clothes and other household goods.

Now there were more people traveling on the road. Most of them were going in the same direction we were going. As we continued southward, more and more people were going in the same direction.

Suddenly, Father stopped, looked, and noticed that the road was going east! He said, "Look, up ahead of us. The wall is turning and is going west! There is a small path going through the break in the wall just like Mr. Hunter said. It is going through the break in the wall and heading south along the wall.

"Mr. Hunter said to go south along the Great Wall of China. He said to follow the wall to the village against the Great Wall. He said that the village is completely surrounded by a tall wall with large gates. The gates are the only way to enter into the village with camels, horses, and wagons.

"All the people are going east. That is the wrong way! That must be another branch of the Silk Road across the Gobi Desert. We need to go south, not east. Mr. Hunter said we must go south along the wall all the way to the village. This road is going east away from the wall."

All the people walking and riding on their camels were going east. Many people traveling in that same direction spoke Russian, Chinese, and Arabic. Father asked one of the Russian-speaking travelers which road went to Lanzhou (Lanchow), China. The man quickly answered my father in fluent Russian as he pointed to a small, sandy path that went south along the Great Wall.

"There. That road there will take you to Lanzhou, China." Before Father had a chance to ask how far it was to Lanzhou, the man was gone. He was apparently walking very fast, trying to catch up with the rest of his group.

We stood there at the crossroads not knowing what to do. Then the first camel driver of a caravan coming from the north looked at us and realized we were confused and didn't know where to go. The camel driver got Father's attention by shouting the word, "Lanzhou" several times and then pointed south and shouted again, "Lanzhou, Lanzhou."

Father said, "Da [Yes]. Lanzhou." The camel driver pointed to the small, sandy, winding path by the wall going south. The camel caravan quickly passed us and continued going south alongside the Great Wall. Father realized that we must follow the caravan south, for that was the direction that we needed to travel.

Our pace temporarily quickened and our hearts were uplifted as we tried to follow and keep up with the camel caravan in front of us. However, we, along with our horses were exhausted and started walking slower instead of faster. The camel caravan quickly blended in with the far horizon and vanished from sight, fusing with the heat waves rising from the hot, sandy surface of the desert, which produces mirages across the Gobi wasteland. Once again, we were left behind to struggle for our lives through the deep, soft, life-taking sand.

We helped our horses by pushing the cart through the sand to keep it from becoming stuck. This was very exhausting for everybody, as well as for the horses. This slowed us down immensely. The horses were struggling, and we were struggling as we pushed the cart to keep it from being stuck in the sand.

Apparently, we had strayed too far from the mountains where the ground was more firm. After struggling for a long time, Father said, "We need to get closer to the mountains. There we'll be able to travel faster where there is less sand and more firm ground. That should make traveling much easier for us and the horses. We will make good time."

We followed the Great Wall as Mr. Hunter had recommended. He was right. In many places, the wall was crumbling down. In other sections, there was no wall. In front of us, the only remaining signs of the wall were piles and piles of rocks in the crumbled-down sections of the wall. These piles of rocks stretched endlessly in front of us. This happened mostly in remote parts of the desert.

There were no villages around these piles of rocks. Because there had been no people living in this region, the wall had not been taken care of for many years. The elements had eroded the wall and had reduced it to nothing but piles of rocks. We started to notice that when the wall was in good repair, there was a village up ahead. The villagers took pride in the Great Wall and rebuilt it when it was crumbling.

Some of the villages along the wall were very small and consisted of five or six huts. Other villages consisted of anywhere from six to ten huts, all plastered against the wall. The huts were constructed so the back wall of the hut was the Great Wall of China. That way they only had to build three more walls, a roof, and a door. The back wall was already built for them, maybe a thousand years before they had settled there. History tells us that remnants of the Great Wall of China had been in construction around 300 BC.

Throughout the centuries, each kingdom had built on the wall. Many sections of the wall in the eastern Xinjiang (Sinkiang) province were crumbling. In the northern Gansu province, the wall was crumbling as well. There had been no people living in that area at that time, and as a result, nobody had taken an interest in rebuilding the wall.

Now China is proud of the Great Wall. It has been rebuilt and is a world tourist attraction. Today, the Great Wall snakes its way across the continent of China for 13,170 miles. It is one of the Seven Wonders of the World and can be seen from space.

The road seemed to meander between the piles of rocks. First, the road was on one side of the rocks and the wall. Then it was on the other side of the wall, running parallel with it. It reminded us of a giant snake slithering on the ground across the countryside and around the big piles of rocks.

As we continued south, we did not see the wall any longer. We followed the piles of rocks that used to be the wall. After walking all day and seeing nothing but piles of rocks on the side of road where the wall should have been, we wondered if we had wandered off course and were going in the wrong direction.

Toward nightfall, we started seeing the wall again. Now we knew we were on the right road. As darkness set in, Father found a nice low spot against the wall. The low spot was to protect us from the strong wind. We would bring the cart and the horses to the low area, unhitch the horses, and make them comfortable. We would huddle together very tightly, trying to keep warm.

We had three things to help keep us warm—we had the shelter afforded by the low spot against the wall, the wall going northeast, and our two-wheeled cart and the horses behind us. In this way, we were getting as much protection as possible from the strong, cold desert wind.

Mother and the infant were in the center. The older children, including me, were around Mother. Father and the oldest three children sat on the outside of the circle. In this manner, the youngest one, with mother, was protected the most from the cold. The people in the outer circle would receive the brunt of the cold night wind blowing across the desert. Therefore, we gave them more clothes so they could stay warm.

By early dawn, we put all of our things on the cart and started walking again. Winter was setting in. We were expecting snow any day. Therefore, Father made haste. He said, "We must keep moving as quickly as we can. We do not want to be caught in the snow in the desert. We must hurry. If we go quickly south, there may be no snow there. It may be warmer there."

We continued to walk fast toward the south for many days. It was getting very cold. Because we were always short of food and water, the trip was very difficult. Now we had another obstacle facing us—the winter cold. We were not prepared for cold weather. We had very few clothes for everybody in our family. Father said, "We have reached the place where the wall turns west. Here we must go through the break in the wall and continue going south. Mr. Hunter said from this point where the wall goes west, we must go south. From this point where the wall goes west, it is about twenty days walking to Jiayuguan Village."

We continued on our journey south. Father said, "We are all getting very tired and weak. Our horses are very tired. We are walking much slower now than before. We do not know if we have enough food for us and the horses for twenty days. We must ration our food supplies so that we will have enough to last us at least twenty days." He said that he still had five combs left. "We will trade our combs for food like we did before when we had no food. These people liked our combs because they are made out of animal horns and are very strong. They do not break like the wooden combs that they have. These people have thick, coarse hair, and the wooden combs just don't last. That is why they like our combs. They don't break, and they last a long time."

We followed the piles of rocks, which gradually came closer together and eventually formed a small, low wall. As we walked along, the wall became wider, taller, and more solidified. We were so happy to see the wall, because it meant that there might be a village ahead of us. There we could trade our combs for food. We also would find rest and shelter for the night.

Our hopes were shattered as we continued to walk along the wall and watched it diminish into piles of rocks as far as our eyes could see. This meant that there was no village ahead of us. There was no chance of getting food or finding shelter for the night. We kept walking until we were out in the open again, with no protection from the cold north wind.

Still, we continued walking until it became too dark to see where we were going. A short distance in front of us, there was a big pile of rocks where the wall used to be. Father headed for those rocks. Then he led the horses, which were pulling the cart, behind the pile of rocks to get some shelter from the cold, winter wind.

Tony and Benny unhitched the horses and tied them to the cart, and we huddled between the rocks and the cart to stay warm. We had no clothes to speak of except what was on our backs. We only had several old, torn blankets in the cart. They were dirty, dusty, and full of holes, but we didn't care. To us, those blankets, no matter how old or dirty they were, were worth their weight in gold. They kept us from freezing to death during the cold winter nights.

We had no food for our horses or us. We could not sleep because we were very hungry and cold. It was so cold that night, even huddling together did not keep us warm. As we huddled closer together, we felt each other shivering from the cold.

We positioned ourselves as close to Mother as we could to stay warm and to keep her and the baby warm. Each person sat sideways with one shoulder toward the inner circle and one shoulder out. All night long, we turned from one side to the other side to keep warm. It was just too cold to sleep.

At the same time anxiously waiting for the dawn to come so we could start walking again to stay warm.

As soon as it was light enough to see, Tony and Benny hitched the horses to the cart, and the rest of us put our two, small, dirty, torn pillows and several dirty, flea-filled blankets in the cart. We also placed a sack of corn on the cart for the horses, which we always tried to get from the villagers as we traveled. We traded our combs for flatbread and the corn. These were the combs that father made and saved for the journey. We were able to get water from the wells along the Silk Road. Mother did not forget to put her pot on the cart as well. She always had that pot with her. Sometimes the water was not drinkable, and we had to boil it. So the pot was always a very useful utensil to have.

Before we started walking, we took our hats off and prayed. We thanked God for the safety of our journey thus far, for the food, and the rest to our bodies. We prayed for wisdom, guidance, and most of all, His will to be done. After Father's prayer, we felt encouraged, energized, cheerful, and ready to continue on our journey to wherever He led us.

By early afternoon, we encountered the Great Wall again. It appeared to be rebuilt and well taken care of. We also encountered more travelers now. There were many camel caravans coming and going. We felt more confident now, as we knew we were approaching a village.

The camel drivers from the caravans waved at us as they passed us coming and going. We were walking very slowly. We had been walking most of the morning. We were hungry, cold, and tired. Our horses were tired as well. The camels were more than twice the size of our horses and had big, flat feet. They walked in the sand as if it were hard ground. Nothing slowed them down in the desert.

On the other hand, our horses were small and their hooves were sinking in the soft sand as they walked and pulled the cart. They struggled as they tried to pull the cart through the sand. Many times when the sand was too soft, our cart would get bogged down. All of us would push the cart to help the horses.

Father said to us, "This is the twenty-fourth day that we have been on the road since we left Mr. Hunter in the Gobi Desert. Remember, he said that it would take about twenty five days to reach the village? This must be the village where Mr. Hunter said that we must sell our horses and the cart and travel by truck to Lanzhou, China."

Chapter 41

Danger near the Walled
Jiayuquan Village

It was early afternoon as we continued to walk and at times, to push the cart to keep it from becoming stuck in the sand. Father said, "If we hurry, we can reach the village just before dark."

Shortly after he made that statement, we caught up to the camel driver, who had just passed us. He had apparently realized that we were in a rush to make it to the village by nightfall, because he had stopped and had waited for us to catch up to him. He spoke in Arabic and waved his arms frantically for us to keep going. Since Tava, Tony, and Benny spoke Arabic, he explained to them that we must spend the night here in the desert away from the village.

He said, "It is too dangerous for you to approach the village at night alone. The gates will be closed, and you'll be forced to spend the night outside the village walls. There is much danger there. The robbers will kill you and take everything from you. Therefore, you must spend the night here in the desert, away from the village, and get an early start in the morning. That way you will arrive at the village gates at midday and will be escorted into the village by camel caravans.

"In the Gobi Desert, on the Silk Road, the news travels very fast. All the camel caravans on the Silk Road are aware of your family traveling across the Gobi Desert with only two horses and the two-wheeled cart, with seven children walking. This desert is not for horses. It is for camels.

"All the camel drivers along the route of the Silk Road are amazed that you have survived this long with your two horses, cart, and the seven small children walking. It must be the will of Allah that you and your family are still alive! The Silk Road across the Gobi Desert is designed only for camels, not horses. This is camel country. Horses die here.

"Allah has spared your lives and protected you in the Gobi Desert. We will obey Allah and protect you as you travel across the Gobi. May Allah go with you as you go forward on your destination.

"The camel drivers are aware of your family traveling across the Gobi. They will watch and escort you into Jiayuquan Village safely. Bandits attack only the lone travelers. They will not attack you while you're traveling with a caravan approaching the village. These bandits are ruthless. They have no mercy. They will kill every one of you. They will kill you, and they will kill your children. They will take your horses, your cart, and your clothes. They will leave your bodies to the fate of the desert and the wild animals."

He once again stressed to us in Arabic that we must spend the night here in the desert away from the village, saying, "Do not approach the village by yourselves. It is too dangerous. Robbers will kill you before you can get close to the village gates. Robbers have no mercy, they will kill all your children and kill you and take everything you have. You must spend the night here in the desert. It is safer for you. You are about half a day's walk from Jiayuquan Village.

"In the morning you must travel into the village with a caravan, not by yourselves. Tomorrow there will be many caravans going into the village. They all know who you are and how you have traveled and survived the Silk Road with horses instead of camels. They will escort you safely into the village!

"It must be the will of Allah that your family and your horses are still alive. Nobody survives in the Gobi walking with children and old horses pulling a two-wheeled cart. Tomorrow morning the camel caravans will escort you and give you protection into Jiayuquan Village."

Taking the advice of the camel driver, we got off the road, found a nice low spot against the wall, and rested. When darkness came, we spent another freezing night in the desert by the Great Wall of China. We huddled together, shivering and trying to keep as warm as possible with our old, torn blankets. Everybody wanted to be covered by a piece of the blanket, so everybody huddled even closer together around Mother and the infant. We kept them warm in the center as we leaned against her and used the pieces of blankets to cover the backs of the people sitting on the outside of the circle. All of us had a restless night.

By dawn, we heard the camel caravans traveling on the road. We hurriedly got our things together and threw them into the two-wheeled cart. In the meantime, Father, Tony, and Benny hitched the horses to the cart.

By daybreak, we were well on our way to the village. Mother walked with Father. She said that the little baby was very sick. He responded, "We will get help in the village. We will seek out a doctor or try to get medicine for him!"

The camel caravans passed us coming and going as if we were standing still in the sand. Our two old horses were struggling to pull the cart across the deep sand. Many times our cart would become bogged down in the sand. Then all of us would pitch in and push it out of the sand. The horses continued to pull the cart slowly. By noon, we were approaching the village.

This was a very large settlement. The entire village was surrounded by a big wall, which was almost a continuation of the Great Wall of China. The only way in and out of the village for wagons, carts, and big animals was the huge gates through which we would be escorted into the village. These gates closed at sundown and opened after daylight.

There was a small gate on the side of the big gate that remained unlocked all night. This was called the Needle Gate. It was large enough for only one person to go through at a time.

The Bible says, "It is easier for a camel to go through the eye of a needle, than for a rich man to enter into the kingdom of God" (Mark 10:25). It is referring to the small gate in the Jerusalem city wall.

Only small animals like sheep or goats can squeeze through it one at a time. This small gate is basically for goat and sheep herders. Sometimes the herdsman cannot gather their herd fast enough before the main gates close, so they go through the Needle Gate to get inside the village after dark. Other people use the Needle Gate as well to go in and out of the village.

Many caravans were coming into the village and others were going out of the village. We ended up in the middle of a caravan as we approached the village—half the caravan was in front of us and the other half was behind us. The caravan slowed its pace to match our pace as we walked beside our cart.

The camel drivers did not communicate verbally but somehow already knew what to do to give us protection. These frequent travelers on the Silk Road were quite aware of all the dangers that existed just outside the village walls. They knew how to protect themselves and others from the danger in a desert. They escorted us and protected us from the danger outside the walls of the village.

As we walked through the village gates with the big camel caravan, the camel drivers were very happy. They were smiling and waving at us as they rode off in one direction and pointed for us to go the other way into the village. We stood there and watched the caravan move farther away from us. We didn't know what to say. We were speechless. We were inside the village and were safe!

Father broke the silence by saying, "Let us pray and thank God for our health, for the safety of the trip, and for the caravan that led us safely into the village. Let us pray that His will shall be done through all of this." Now, Father understood what the camel driver had told us a long time ago, "We take care of each other here in the Gobi Desert. We depend on and we need each other in the desert."

After we finished praying, we continued to stand there watching the caravan that had helped us blend in with other camel caravans and disappear into the crowded village market. We were so overwhelmed by the assistance from this camel caravan that we felt like part of our family just rode off and left us.

We were so engrossed while watching our caravan disappear that we didn't notice or hear a familiar voice behind us. "Ah, we meet again, Mr. Peter," Mr. Chiu commented, as he approached us from behind and put his arm on my father's shoulder. Mr. Chiu, embracing my father, thanked him again for letting him and his son walk with us. He thanked us for sharing our food with him and his son as we had walked together for several days crossing communist territory.

"Mr. Peter, I did not tell you when we met you walking from Kuldja that we had not eaten for two days nor had any water for two days. My son and I were dying from dehydration and starvation. We did not know if we could have survived another day. Then you and your family came along and shared with us what little food and water that you had to help us. Thank you so much for your generosity and kindness for helping us.

"Here, my family and I are together again. We have you to thank for it. Without food and water, we would not have survived the journey. All the time, we feared for our lives. We did not know whether we would see another day or if we would be caught and executed or die from starvation.

"Your God sent you to rescue me and my son from certain death. My family and I want to thank you for helping me and my son in the desert. I heard you several times praying to your God while we were on the road. You prayed and thanked your God for the safety of the trip, for the food, and for the friends. You have very strong faith in your God! It was your God who led us to you so you could help us to continue our journey safely to our home."

He continued, "We parted ways after crossing the river separating free China and communist China. My son and I went southeast with our friends. You and your family went northeast. Now, we meet again under different circumstances. Jiayuguan Village is my home! My people lived in this village for many generations.

There are many stories told about a stranger from another country called Marco Polo, who traveled and many times, stayed in this village. He was a very important man. He was a foreigner that traveled the Silk Road, which goes through this village. This village was one of the big oases on the Silk Road. He was a very trusted envoy for many years in the foreign dominated court of Kublai Kahn. Yes, Marco Polo traveled and lived in my village many years ago. Today he comes to life, as our grandparents tell us about all of his travels and about his strong devotion and service to Kublai Kahn.

"When my son and I arrived here and walked through the main [west] gate with the caravan, nothing was changed. The wall, the main west gate, and the sections of the wall were crumbling down. This is the historical gate through which all the criminals and disgraced officials were banished. Through this gate [gate to hell], they were forced out to face and battle the western wilderness of the merciless Gobi Desert. Here their lives were snuffed out, and they became nothing more than a handful of sand scattered across the Gobi by the violently raging desert sand storms!"

You will see a picture of a frequent, unexpected, unpredictable, blinding sand and dust storm in the Gobi Desert.

16. Photo of typical dust and sand storms in that region of the world

17. Photo of camels going through the break
in the wall near Jiayuguan pass

"This is my village and my home! Here, in Jiayuquan village, I have friends and contacts in high places. We will help you as much as we can.

"Mr. Peter, you must sell your horses and your two-wheeled cart here in Jiayuquan Village. You cannot travel with a cart and horses from here to Lanzhou, China. There are very big mountains and dangerous roads from here to Lanzhou. Only trucks can travel from here to Lanzhou. I will help you buy tickets on the truck to transport you and your family to Lanzhou. In Lanzhou, there are American missionaries who will help you to settle there, or if you need to go farther, they will help you.

Mr. Peter, you asked me about a doctor for your sick son. Well there are no doctors and no medicine in the village. Fear of Communism even reached this village. All the doctors fled from here for fear of being executed!"

Mr. Chiu stayed with us, and after several days, was finally able to help Father sell the horses and the cart. The money that we received was not enough to buy tickets to ride the truck to Lanzhou (Lanchow).

Mr. Chiu found an empty room and told us to wait there for several days while he got more money for the tickets. The room had no doors, just an open doorframe. The windows were pasted with paper to keep the cold out. There was no glass in the windows, just paper. Some hay was in a corner of the room, so we made ourselves comfortable in the hay on the dirt floor. There was no source of heat or light in the room other than a light coming through the open doorway. It was very cold but not as cold as outside.

Toward late afternoon, Mr. Chiu came with a man. He introduced the man to my father and said, "This is the driver of the truck that will take you to Lanzhou. He knows where the American missionaries live in Lanzhou. I know this driver and trust him. He will take you to the American missionaries. He also fled from communism in Kuldja. Only he survived and was able to escape. His entire family was slaughtered by the communists in Kuldja."

Mr. Chiu added that he had paid the landlord for the use of the room for as long as we needed to stay there—until we left on the truck to Lanzhou (Lanchow). "Do not worry. Nobody will chase you out of this room. Mr. Peter, you and your family rest well. You have a very long journey ahead of you on the truck." Mr. Chiu laughingly remarked as he was walking out with the driver, "Sleeping in this room is much better than sleeping outside in the cold and also riding the truck will be much better than walking in the desert in the cold days and nights." Mr. Chiu and the driver quickly walked out of the room and disappeared around the corner. We never saw or heard from Mr. Chiu again.

Late that afternoon, a well-dressed man with a servant came to the doorway of the room where we stayed. He said that Mr. Chiu sent him to make sure that we had everything we needed before we started the long, cold journey to Lanzhou. He looked at our family and then focused his attention on us children. He said, "You are very fortunate people that you have a friend like Mr. Chiu to help you. Mr. Chui's sister is a personal friend of the governor's wife of the province of Gansu. Mr. Chiu, through his sister, was able to present your case to the governor of Gansu Province. And that is how they were able to get money to help pay for the trip to Lanzhou."

Chapter 42

Problems with the Truck

Benny, my older brother, woke me up in the middle of the night and said, "Look out the door. It is snowing. That's why it is so cold." We huddled together on the hay in a corner of the room, trying to stay as warm as possible. There was no door, just a doorframe. Still it was not as cold as it was when we were sleeping in the desert by the Great Wall of China. We had no wind blowing against us in this room, however, it was still very cold. We huddled together, shivering and trying to stay warm.

At dawn, the driver walked in and said, "We must go now. The truck is waiting, and there are many people that want to ride the truck. You and your family must sit directly behind the cab in the back. It will be much warmer there. It will be much safer there for the children. Don't let the people push you away. You stay behind the cab where I will seat you. Do not move from that spot. That will be the safest and warmest place in the back of the truck. You will have protection from the strong wind. I also will be looking back through my little window to make sure that you are okay and that nobody pushed you away from that spot.

"Mr. Chiu said that you are special people, and that I must take good care of you. I know the American missionaries in Lanzhou, the Schoerners. I will take you to them."

Carrying the small bundles of clothes that we had with us, we approached the truck. We noticed that there were many people surrounding the truck and that all of them wanted to ride the truck to Lanchow. They were being persecuted for their beliefs and now they also were fleeing from communism. All of them were fleeing for their lives. These people were from all walks of life—farmers, merchants, shop owners, homeowners, wealthy people, and business people. All these people had nothing with them except the clothes on their backs and a few items that they were able to carry with them. The communists had stripped them of all their belongings, their land, their homes, their money, and their jewelry. The communists spared their lives only if they left with the clothes on their backs and a few cheap trinkets that they were allowed to carry with them. Those who refused to part with their belongings, such as jewelry, money, expensive clothes, fur coats, homes, and land, were executed on the spot and everything that belonged to them was taken.

From the looks of the crowd, we needed about twenty trucks to take all of these people to Lanzhou. The driver allowed only those people who had tickets to get on the truck. He would take a ticket from each person and carefully match the name on the ticket with the name on his list. He would then double-check that the ticket matched up with the person. Only then would he allow that person to get on the truck.

The driver spoke in a different Chinese dialect that we did not understand. He waved his arms to indicate that he wanted all the people to back away from the truck. Taking the tickets from my father, he helped Mother and the baby to get into the truck, which was a flatbed with only sideboards and no tailboard. He helped the rest of the children get into the back of the truck. Then Father got into the truck.

We were all packed in there like sardines. When everybody was on board, the truck driver said, "We will go now." It was daylight, and the main gates of the village were opened as we approached them. It felt so different to be riding on the back of a truck instead of walking and pushing the cart across the sand.

The truck was obviously overloaded, and we could hear the motor straining to keep the truck moving as we slowly made the uphill climb.

Suddenly, the truck stopped and the motor went quiet. The driver came out from the front and said, "We must get out and push the truck back into the village. The motor is broken. We must repair it before we can continue the journey."

So all the men got out and pushed the truck back into the village to be repaired. We went into the same cold, empty room and waited. Finally, the driver came and reported that the truck would not be ready for several days. We spent several more cold nights and days waiting for the truck to be repaired.

When the truck was repaired, the driver took us back to the truck and seated us behind the cab as he had done the first time. As we sat there, the rest of the people got into the truck. When everybody was in the truck, it was daylight and the village gates opened. Once again, we drove out of the village going uphill on the winding road toward Lanzhou.

We did not get very far before the truck stopped again and the motor went silent. The driver came around to the back and said, "We must get out and push the truck back into the village and have it repaired again."

This problem with the truck continued to recur for many more days. Once again, the truck was back in the village, and the driver and the mechanics were working on the motor. They said they would have the truck ready in several days, and we would be able to continue our journey.

We went back to our room. We huddled in the hay in the warmest corner of the room where there was less cold wind blowing through the doorway. It seemed like it was much colder than the previous nights. The cold wind was blowing the snow into the room. When the cold wind died down, we felt more comfortable and warm.

Chapter 43

Our Baby Brother Dies

In the middle of the twelfth night, Mother woke us up and said that Nikki, our little brother, was dying. We huddled around Mother and the infant, closer and closer, as we listened to his last few breaths. Then there was total silence. We edged closer, straining to hear some sounds from him, but there was nothing. I thought maybe he was holding his breath and would start breathing again shortly, but no, he didn't start breathing again. He did not make any more sounds.

Out of the clear blue, Nida, my younger sister, asked, "Did God take Nikki from us? Will God take care of Nikki, and will He feed him and keep him warm?"

"Yes, Nida, God will take good care of Nikki. He will always keep him warm and have plenty of food for him. Nikki will never be sick again," Mother answered in a soft, quivering, sobbing voice. When we heard our mother crying, we all cried with her. We were all sad that we lost our little baby brother. However, like mother said, God would take good care of him.

The night seemed to pass very quickly, and it was daylight. Father quickly went and found the driver and told him what had happened. He told him that we must bury Nikki here before we could go on. The driver understood and said he would wait for us.

Father took Tony, Benny, Alex, and me out the small side gate of the village to find a place to bury Nikki. We went up the hill along the wall and found a soft place against the Great Wall of China where the ground was not frozen solid. The rocks were loose, so we moved them and dug a hole in the ground big enough to bury Nikki in.

We came back to the room and got Mother, Nikki's body, and the rest of the family. We wrapped Nikki's body with his clothes and his blanket and put him in the hole in the ground against the Great Wall of China, not very far from the main village gate. Then we covered him up with many big rocks. This was to keep the wild animals from digging up Nikki's body.

We prayed by his grave. All of us were crying as we made our way back into the village through the small gate and into our room to wait for the truck.

Father waited for the driver. When he came, Father told him that we were ready to go. The driver got everybody on the truck again, and we started out toward the village gates.

Suddenly, there was a lot of commotion and yelling from the people standing along the side of the street right before the village gate. A man ran out of the crowd, grabbed a screaming child, placed him under his arm like a sack of potatoes, and ran toward the truck, which was moving away. The child was my little brother, Alex, who was screaming at the top of his lungs because he thought he was going to be left behind.

Alex had wandered away toward a group of soldiers, who had been standing on the corner. He had been starving like the rest of us. He had seen the soldiers eating food and had wanted some. Going over to where the soldiers were, he had asked them for some food. They had laughed and had pointed at Alex. One of the soldiers had reached into his pocket, had pulled out some old Chinese coins, and had thrown them on the ground in front of him. You can see a picture of the coins the soldiers gave to Alex and that he has been saving all these years on the next page.

18. Photos of coins given to my little brother,
Alex, by the soldiers in January 1947.

Alex, without hesitation, had gotten on his hands and knees, had
quickly grabbed the coins off the ground, and had shoved them in his
pocket. What Alex had really wanted more than the coins was the food
that they were eating. He had been starving. Just the smell of the food
had made his mouth water. He had kept on making motions to them
that he wanted some food to eat. They had continued to laugh and to
make fun of Alex.

Finally, the soldiers had realized that he was asking for food. They
had looked at each other and had decided to give him some food. The

soldiers had been amazed that he was able to stuff so much food into his small mouth and was already asking for more. While Alex had been preoccupied with stuffing the whole portion, which had been given to him, as fast as he could into his small mouth, he had looked up and had seen the truck start to pull way. Alex had immediately dropped the food and had started to scream and to run after the truck.

However, his tiny legs had not been able to move his body fast enough to catch up with the moving truck. That had been when a man had rushed out of the crowd, had grabbed the screaming little boy, and had started running with him toward the truck. That is when we realized that Alex was missing and all the commotion was about my little brother, who screamed as he was brought to the truck by the stranger.

By now, the truck driver heard the commotion and knew that something was wrong. He stopped the truck and got out to see what the problem was. About that time, he saw a man running toward the truck with a screaming child under his arm. All the people on the truck reached out to help. Three men on the very back of the truck reached down and grabbed Alex from the man who had been running with him. Once the people on the truck got their hands on the scared little boy, they grabbed him and pulled him onto the back of the truck. Now the people in the truck motioned for the truck driver to go forward.

The truck driver got back in his truck and started driving toward the village gates and up the winding hill toward the steep, high, rugged mountains as we headed toward Lanchow. Our journey continued for about two weeks through these rugged mountains.

We established a routine. All able-bodied men and women pushed the truck uphill and rode it downhill. This happened daily as we slowly made our way on the winding road through the rugged mountains.

We all had mixed emotions. We were thrilled that we were riding on the back of a truck instead of walking as we had been for many months. However, we were very sad that we had lost our little baby brother and had buried him next to the Great Wall of China. Some of us stood silently with tears in our eyes. Others were speechless. Father did not cry, but we knew he was hurting inside. He tried not to show it. The tone of his voice was lower, softer, and quieter than usual. Mother was also hurting and was very sad.

Many times, we would look up at Mother and see her crying. We tried our best to comfort her in her sorrow, but we could not understand the depth of it. Father understood her sorrow but didn't know how to express it to us so we could understand.

We prayed a lot after Nikki passed away. Father always assured us in his prayers that Nikki was happy and well cared for by God. If we somehow could have kept him alive until we got on the truck, maybe with all the people sitting close together, we could have kept him warm. Maybe some of those people would have given us food for him to make him stronger and to fight his infection. Then he would still be with us riding on the way to Lanchow.

Chapter 44

Public Toilets

We traveled south on the back of the flatbed truck, which had no tarp and no tailgate. Only the sideboards were there to keep people from falling off the truck. We were still in a dry, mountainous region. As usual, we would push the truck uphill and ride downhill. We encountered many small villages along the way.

Rest stops were infrequent but occurred at least two to three times a day. While still in remote areas of the desert, we would relieve ourselves behind the truck, a rock, or wherever was available. As the villages became larger, public restrooms were available.

One restroom, which my older brother, Benny, took me to in one village was a typical restroom for a smaller village. Was it unique? Yes. It was very unique. It consisted of one large room with a slightly elevated platform, which ran lengthwise from one side of the room to the other. The platform was three feet wide and eight inches high.

All you had to do was find an empty slot, step up on the platform, turn around, drop your pants, squat down, and let her rip. In more specific terms, you had to step up on the platform, turn around, drop your pants, crouch or squat down, and push as hard as you could, making sure that your gold fell away from the elevated platform that you were crouching on. You had to hang over the edge and push as hard as you could so your own feces wouldn't fall into your pants but would be propelled away from the elevated platform that you were standing on.

If you were good at it and could push hard, you could accomplish your mission and be relieved. You might even be clean too.

Oh, by the way, there was no such thing as toilet paper. You brought what you had with you and did the best you could with it. You cleaned yourself up the best you could. After that, the job was done.

What happened when the trough filled with human gold? Simple, it was recycled! The waste was taken out of the trough and placed into baskets. Farmers carried the full baskets out into the fields where they were used to fertilize their gardens—you know, to fertilize the vegetables that you eat. Is that cool or what? That country knew how to recycle well. Remember, this was the desert. There was no water and no waste, therefore, everything was recycled.

Chapter 45

William Borden Memorial Hospital in Lanchow, China

I looked at my parents as we were rode in the back of the truck and noticed that they were praying. We children also started to pray that the truck would not break down again and that we would continue on our journey. To our surprise and amazement, the truck did not break down.

We rode the truck over steep mountain passes and narrow roads. Toward nightfall, we stopped and rested. People walked around the truck to stretch their legs and arms.

Almost every day, all the men were asked to get out of the truck and to push it uphill. The truck was not able to carry the big load up the hill. Once on top of the hill, the men would get back in, and we would ride the truck downhill. This type of a routine occurred at least two to three times a day—in between the truck's breakdowns. The men were always ready to push the truck up the hill.

We passed many more villages, which were closer together now—at least it seemed that way because we were riding in the truck and were moving much faster than we had been when we were walking. The truck's driver took special care of us and saw that we had a place to stay at night. Early in the morning, he would put us back behind the cab of the truck in the same spot where he could see us through the little window in the cab. After that, the rest of the people would get on the truck, and we would continue the journey once more.

We had been riding and pushing the truck for about fourteen days when we finally came to Lanchow, China. Father said, "Here we will meet more missionaries who will help us. I have the letter in my pocket that George Hunter gave to me to give to the missionaries. These missionaries are from America. They will know how to help us when we get to Lanchow."

By midday of the fourteenth day riding on the back of the flatbed truck, we arrived at the city of Lanchow, China. Upon entering the city, half of the people got off the truck the first time it stopped. The rest of the people got off the second time the truck stopped because there was a bus stop and a train station there. They were gone within a few minutes. We were alone on the truck.

The truck driver, looking at my father, said in Russian with a strong Chinese accent, "You and the family stay on the truck. I will take you to the American missionaries, and they will help you." The driver got back into the truck and drove us clear across town. He drove across a big bridge, turned, and drove back along the opposite side, the north side, of the Yellow River. After driving for two more miles, he pulled up to the William Borden Memorial Hospital Compound in Lanchow, China.

This is where the Schoerner family lived. This is where Mr. and Mrs. Schoerner did their missionary work. Mr. Schoerner worked in the hospital as the business administrator. This was their base of operations for the mission work in Gansu Province and beyond.

William Borden Memorial Hospital in Lanchow, China, had been built after the death of William Borden on April 9, 1913. William Borden, the son and heir of the multi-million-dollar, famous Borden Dairy Estate in Chicago, had graduated from Yale University in 1909 and later had graduated from Princeton Theological Seminary.

William had written to his mother stating that God was calling him to be a missionary to the Muslim people in China. One friend had expressed amazement that William would throw his life away by renouncing his father's entire fortune to become a lowly missionary in China and serving God by ministering to the Muslim people in northwestern wilderness of China.

On the way to the mission field, William had stopped in Cairo, Egypt, to study the Arabic language in order to be better prepared to work with the Muslim people. While in Egypt, William had contracted cerebral meningitis and had died in Cairo during his training at the age of twenty-five.

The Borden family had bequeathed one million dollars to China Inland Missions and to other Christian organizations. The Borden Memorial Hospital in Lanchow had been built and had been named after William Whiting Borden. Today, William Borden Memorial Hospital still stands, surrounded by a massive medical complex. The central portion of the complex is the heart of the institution that is called William Borden Memorial Hospital, which is the historical origin of this institution.

19. Lanzhou by Yellow River

As the truck approached the yard, a man and a woman came out of the house and waved at the truck driver. The truck pulled up to the house, and the driver got out and approached the couple. They all bowed as they greeted one another. After a brief exchange of words between the driver and the couple, the driver pointed at us, and we assumed these were the American missionaries. The lady motioned for us to get down from the truck. The truck driver and Father helped all the children and Mother to get off the truck. Then the truck driver and the couple exchanged farewells, bowed to each other, and the driver got in the truck and drove off.

We stood there, not knowing what to do. Father said, "Well, here we are in Lanchow, China. These must be the American missionaries that Mr. Hunter was telling us about. I still have the letter that Mr. Hunter gave me to give to them." Just as Father was reaching into his pocket for the letter, the missionary couple approached us and introduced themselves as Mr. and Mrs. Schoerner. They said that they were American missionaries from Moody Bible Institute in Chicago, America.

As we looked at the missionaries in front of us and they looked at us, we wondered what they were thinking as they saw our poor, destitute family seeking refuge and freedom to worship God. At this point, we were exhausted, weary, dirty, and hungry and had dirty, torn, and patched clothes. These were the same clothes we had been wearing when we left Kuldja about eight months before that. The only difference was that now these clothes were full of holes, patches, fleas, and lice.

Father showed them the letter that Mr. George Hunter had written to them from the Gobi Desert in northern China and southern Mongolia where he had ministered to the people for many years. The missionaries took and read the letter immediately. Upon reading the letter, they could not believe that we had walked across Northern China and across parts of the Gobi Desert in northwestern China and Mongolia with eight children and the two-wheeled cart pulled by two old horses.

This was on the southern edge of the Gobi Desert. We had lost our youngest sibling in the Gobi Desert from cold, disease, and starvation.

The missionaries took a second look at us and immediately started talking among themselves. We did not understand English, so sign language became very important to us. We learned very quickly how to use our hands when we wanted something or explained something. We also started to pick up one or two words in English.

Mrs. Schoerner took each one of us in a room where we were told to undress, and she scrubbed each one of us in the tub. Then she gave us clean clothes to wear. Mr. Schoerner took a long stick, picked up our clothes with it, took them outside, and placed them in a pile. He made sure that he did not touch any of the clothes. He took some kerosene and poured it all over our clothes. I thought he was pouring a special solution to clean our clothes before washing them, but he lit a match and tossed it into the pile of our clothes. All of our clothes were burning. As I looked at our clothes burning, I stood there feeling confused and crying.

I could not understand why he was burning our good clothes. We wore and lived in these same good clothes for about eight months without taking them off. We had no second set of clothes to wear. What we had on our backs was what we wore through the entire journey up until now. It was very confusing.

It was only later that I found out the reason he had burned our clothes. Father told me all the clothes had been infested with lice and fleas. The only way to get rid of the lice and fleas had been to burn the clothes. The clothes had been very old and had had nothing but patches and holes in them. After almost a year of living and sleeping in the same set of clothes, God, through his servants, had given us some new clothes to wear.

God also sent a missionary family to help us. The Schoerner family was a gift from heaven. They gave us clothes, food, and shelter. They shared everything that they had with us. The missionaries found a house for us to rent, which was close to where they lived. That way we stayed in close contact with them. They were always there, trying to help us.

There was a language barrier. We did not speak English, and the Schoerners did not speak Russian, but they understood some Arabic. Tava, Tony, and Benny understood Arabic quite well. Chinese was out of the question—the Chinese dialect in Lanchow was different from the dialect in Kuldja. Eventually, we were able to communicate quite well. We were learning a few words in English, and they were learning a few words in Russian.

The missionaries tried to get jobs for my father and my mother. They would take my parents to various places to find new positions for them. With my parents' inability to speak Chinese or English, they were at a big disadvantage and were only able to find work housecleaning or washing clothes for other people. We were grateful for that because it put food on the table for the family.

Those jobs were temporary in nature. Mr. Schoerner and Father would regularly go to Lanchow to look for work for my father. Many times, instead of walking a mile along the riverbank to the other bridge, which had not been destroyed by the communists, and walking back on the other side to Lanchow proper, Mr. Schoerner and Father would cross the Yellow River on pigskin rafts.

People were ferried across the river on rafts for a nominal fee. The rafts were made out of pigskins. Because the skin of a pig is very thick, they took it off the body, tied all the openings closed, and blew it up like a balloon. They would take about six or eight of these inflated pigskin balloons and would tie them together. Then they placed boards on top of the inflated pigskins and secured them with ropes. They were called "pigskin rafts."

Crossing on a raft was much quicker than walking along the riverbank to the bridge, crossing the bridge, and walking back on the other side of the river. So the pigskin rafts became a very efficient way of crossing the Yellow River to go into Lanchow proper. Pigskin rafts are still used in remote areas of China. They are also used in larger cities as a tourist attraction for those who want an unusual activity and to experience the past.

We prayed regularly with the missionaries. Finally, we came to the conclusion that we must move on to where there was a Russian community. There we could fit in and could do more work for the Lord. While the parents of both families figured out what we needed to do and how we needed to do it, the kids wandered over the riverbanks and around the countryside.

In the morning, we children would go to the riverbank and walk along the river. Many times, we would come across a body that had washed ashore. The missionaries explained to us that it was a common thing to see along the river. These were the bodies of people who had committed suicide because they had been too deep in debt or had lost a job and could not survive. Many of these people had committed suicide because that was the honorable way to die.

Lanchow, 1951 - just before returning to the U.S.A.

20. Photo of the Schoerner family taken in front of their home in Lanchow, in Gansu Province at the Borden Memorial Hospital compound where they lived and worked

21. Photo of my older sister Lydia holding Bill Shoerner in her lap in Lanzhou, China, April, 1947. This is one of the sons that I corresponded with during the time I wrote this book.

22. Photo of the Shelohvostoff family in Lanchow, China, after we were cleaned up and had new clothes. Thanks to the Schoerner family, who were missionaries from Moody Bible Institute in Chicago and missionaries in that region of China.

Chapter 46

Shanghai Bound

After living for about two-and-a-half months in a house provided by the Shoerners, Father and Brother Schoerner looked for employment for my father, who was a foreigner and did not speak Chinese or English, but they were unsuccessful. Father became very discouraged and stated that Lanzhou was not where God wanted us to do his work. We felt we needed to continue our journey until God told us to stop!

My father was again becoming very restless. He kept saying that we must go, but where? We did not know. He insisted that we needed to finish God's journey that He had set before us.

Mr. and Mrs. Schoerner said there was a very large Russian community in Shanghai and that they had missionary friends from America who were there, working among the Russian people. They would write a letter to the Russian Baptist Church about us. Their missionary friends in Shanghai would help us get situated among the Russian people. We should go to the Russian Baptist Church in Shanghai and show them the letter asking for assistance for our family.

Here is a copy of the letter that Mrs. Anna Schoerner wrote to the Russian Baptist Church in Shanghai, on May 19, 1947, from Lanchow, China.

China Inland Mission,
Lanchow,Kansu, China.
May 19,1947.

This is to introduce a family of Russian Christians
who half a year ago left Sinkiang.Mr Shellachvostov
was a Russian Baptist pastor for a number of years
preceeding 1931 in Siberia.About the time several of
the other fellow pastors of his group were made to
disappear and being warned that the same fate awaited
him he made his escape with his family over into Sinkiang. There he settled in the Ili valley where there
is quite a colony of Russian refugees and a great number of whom were Christians.The Baptist church there
had a pastor but this brother used to assist with the
church work in an honorary capacity.Last year the
leaders of this little church were made to disappear
and at the same time agents from their old home country
pressed the church members to sign up as citizens for
their protection.Many,feeling this would be the end of
their religious freedom,refused to do this but also
were sure that they could no longer stay in Ili.They
have been coming out in flocks.The American Consul in
Tihwa is a Christian and sympathetic and has helped these
Christian refugees obtain passes for travel into Kansu
This family likely was immune to very great persecution
due to their very evident poverty.Owners of property
were made to suffer more.They had a long winter journey
here to Lanchow and enroute they lost their youngest
child an infant of seven months.While they have been
here we have done all we could to assist them find work,
living quarters,etc.But Lanchow is a hard place and all
feel that Shanghai will be a better place to find work
and educational advantages for their young folk.The
fact that they do not have much knowledge of the Chinese
languages prejudices any opportu nities for getting employment here in Lanchow.

23. Letter Mrs Anna Schoerner wrote to the Russia
Baptist Church in Shanghai, China

They arrived here with a letter from one of our missionaries who had known them in Sinkiang stating that they were needy and deserving of help. In our few months acquaintance have found them to be good people. The children are well behaved and there is a good spirit of co-operation as a family unit. In spite of their difficulties they have managed to earn from 80 to 90 percent of their living expenses. Used clothing has been donated to them which in these times they could hardly afford or hope to obtain themselves. Everything saleable they sold in Sinkiang to get here and after five months of travel they were in rags.

Mr Shallachvostov has in the past dozen or more years done whatever he can find to do to try to support his growing family. He has some mechanical knowledge and has done some electrical work, photography, soap making, and the like. But here in Lanchow it has not been easy for him. On the other hand his wife and daughter have had no lack of opportunity to take in washing, or go out and work by the day doing cleaning, whitewashing, and laundry work. Mr and Mrs Shellachvostov have been a great help to us in the Christian work among the other Russian speaking refugees. We should very much have liked to have them stay but also realise that their children need better educational opportunities.

We hope that Christian friends along the way will assist this family enroute. They are strangers in a strange land and may run into difficulties along this journey.

Mr and Mrs Otto F. Schoerner

Katharine and Otto F. Schoerner

24. Mrs Schoerner's letter. We needed to move on to Shanghai.

Mr. and Mrs. Schoerner knew that Father was very anxious to leave, so they arranged passage for our family on a truck and then on a train to take us to Shanghai. Before we got on the truck, the two families came together and prayed. Mr. and Mrs. Schoerner prayed in English, and Father and Mother prayed in Russian. My parents thanked them for all their wonderful Christian hospitality. This included the clothes they gave us, the food they provided for us during our stay with them, and most of all, the home with a Christian environment they had provided for a strange family, which had come from the Gobi Desert seeking Christian fellowship and religious freedom from communist persecution.

There were many people on the truck already, but the driver said there was plenty of room for our family. He would squeeze us on the truck without difficulty. After praying together and again thanking the Schoerners for everything, we got on the truck.

The truck headed for Shanghai. As before, we would push the truck uphill and ride it downhill. The people who pushed the truck would end up riding just long enough to get rested up so they could push the truck up the next hill. This was very difficult on all the people who had to push. Because of my crippled leg, they did not make me get out and push. They did leave the little kids on the truck, along with all the belongings that each person had brought with him or her.

We traveled on several trucks. All the people eventually moved from the trucks onto trains. People were leaving northern China in droves. As we were told, this was one of the last opportunities to leave communist China.

For many days, we traveled in a train. People packed into the train car like sardines. As the train car had no seats, people sat on the floor wherever they could find a spot. This train had many boxcars and all of them were packed with people. Huddling together, we tried to stay warm and in one spot during the entire trip. The trip to Shanghai was very difficult. On many days, we encountered delays and derailments, at times, for unknown reasons.

Finally, we arrived at the Shanghai train station, which was packed with all kinds of people speaking various languages. Most of the languages except Russian and Arabic were very strange because we had never heard them before! At the train station, we were met and directed by a guide to go to a refugee camp, along with many other refugee families.

Chapter 47

Refugee Camp in Shanghai

In the refugee center in Shanghai, we were assigned a person who took us to an empty spot the size of a small room. He gave us a tent and told us to set it up. He said that the tent was going to be our home for a long time, so we should make ourselves comfortable and enjoy our stay in Shanghai. He left, and we never saw him again.

Father and the boys set the tent up right away, which was just small enough to fit into the space that had been assigned to us. There was no walking room between our tent and the tents on either side of us. As I went outside and looked around, tents stretched in every direction as far as I could see.

Other people came to our tent and brought us food. The food was American C rations and a gallon-sized, metal sealed can of cheese. I never saw so much cheese in my life. Each day, we were given food for the entire family. As usual, Father got the family together and prayed, thanking God for the safety of the journey thus far, for our new home, for the food, and for all the people that had helped us to get this far on our journey.

After eating our meal one evening, Father said, "We have been in this refugee camp here for almost two months." This was about twelve months from the time we had left Kuldja, Xinjiang, China. "Mother and I have been praying that God would open the doors and show us the way He wants us to go, whether it is God's will for us to stay in Shanghai and minister to the Russian-speaking people or to go elsewhere. We will go where God opens the door for us.

"There are many Russian people and Russian-speaking people in Shanghai as well. Many of them are not saved. If God is willing, we'll stay in Shanghai and minister to all the Russian-speaking people. We must pray that His will shall be done in our lives. He brought us safely thus far, therefore, we are in His Almighty Hands. We will depend on Him to guide us and open the right doors for us. Let us pray again and seek God's guidance. Let us pray and see if God opens the door for us to go to America."

Father said that we were very poor, we could not speak English, we had no friends in America, and we had no money. However, he added, "Let us pray that if it is His will that we go to America, He will provide a way for us to go there. God knows our family, and He knows that we have no resources to reach America. If He wants us to go to America, He will provide a way for us to go.

"We will continue praying that His will may be done, whether God wants us to stay in Shanghai, or He wants us to go to America. We will continue praying, and He will provide the answer for us. We must be patient and let God's will prevail. He has brought us through two countries during wartime, full of death, destruction, disease, and persecution, for believing in God. Through these times of trials and tribulations, He always watched over us as we continuously struggled forward.

"He knows our weaknesses, and He knows our strengths. The will to live and serve God is very strong in our hearts. Thus far, God has provided for us. We must continue to be faithful to him, and He will provide for us in the future as well." Even though the journey was very difficult, Father always prayed and depended on God's almighty power, wisdom, and guidance.

In the refugee camp, they were starting a school to help people learn to read and write in English and Chinese. It seems to me that all the children of school age were separated and placed in different groups. One day, as I sat in class, the teacher pointed at me and motioned for me to stand up. I stood up not knowing what to expect or why the teacher asked me to stand up. The teacher said, "Your name is Yuri Shelohvostoff?"

I answered, "Yes, that is my name."

The teacher asked, "What is this I hear about your father wanting to go to America?"

Responding, I said, "Our family prayed about it."

He replied, "Look at me. I am a professor. I speak several languages. I am fluent in English. I have been in Shanghai for five years waiting for my papers to go to America. I have money and many friends in America. I have people in America who will sponsor me to go there. I'm still here waiting for my papers to go to America.

"Your father, with seven children, no money, no friends in America, who can't speak the language, living in a refugee camp, wants to go to America! Your father is crazy for even thinking about such an idea. Those people who will go to America are those who have money and have connections in America. Even those people have to stand in line and wait for their turn.

"Your father is like a destitute person with seven small children, with no friends in America, doesn't know the language, has no money, and no sponsors to help him. How is your father going to go to America and take his family with him?"

He laughed at me. He thought it was a big joke. He laughed, and the whole class joined him in laughing and making fun of my father for thinking about going to America. As everybody was laughing with the teacher and looking at me, I bowed my head in shame and sat down.

After school, I hobbled home, holding on tightly to my leg to prevent it from collapsing. I dared not look up because I was so ashamed. I knew that everybody looked at me as I hobbled home from school, but I didn't care. I just wanted to get home and hide from all those people who were making fun of me. Once I got home, I crawled into a dark corner of our tent, covered myself with my blanket, and pretended that it was nothing more than just a bad dream.

The next morning, it was business as usual. Everybody got ready to do his or her thing. I felt much better that morning. I was ready to go back to school.

Arriving at school, we were informed that they were taking us to the beach. They put us on a bus, and off we went. The water and the sand were warm. Everybody was playing in the water or sitting on the sand. I wanted to test the water to know how deep it was. I slowly wandered out into deeper water where I was barely touching the bottom with my feet. A small wave would splash against my face and would lift me off the bottom. I felt the strong current pulling my body back and forth when I was unable to touch the bottom. That alone frightened me.

I decided to go back to shallow water. When I was about knee-deep in the water, I felt a strong arm grab my neck and push me under the water. I struggled to break free but could not. I frantically continued to struggle but to no avail. I knew I couldn't hold my breath any longer. I had to come up for air. I knew I would drown unless I could break free and get some air. However, I could not break free from the strong grip that was holding my head down. Whoever was holding me down was much stronger than me.

Just as I was giving up hope and thought I would die, I felt a strong arm reach under my chest and yank me up out of the water. I felt my lungs burning like fire, craving air instead of water. I gasped frantically for air, expecting a mouthful of saltwater to rush into my burning lungs and drown me. To my surprise, the first breath that I took was air instead of water. I immediately felt the burning sensation in my lungs diminish and then disappear as I took my second breath.

When I came to my senses, a boy, who was twice my size, was standing next to me. The Orthodox priest was standing in front of us, holding both of us. He held me up so I would not go underwater and drown. He held onto the other, bigger boy and asked him why he was trying to hold me down. The bigger boy replied, "He's crippled and can't walk normally like everybody else. I wanted to drown him to keep him from suffering!"

The Orthodox priest took me to shore and sat me on the dry sand. He took the other boy away from my area. He continued talking to him for long time. They were too far away for me to hear what he was saying to the boy, who had tried to drown me.

As the day went by, I continued to sit on the beach and tried to recover from the incident where I almost lost my life at the hands of another. I had lost my desire to go into the water. I just wanted to sit there. With my eyes closed, I enjoyed the sunshine, the warm sand, and the warm, salty breeze coming off the ocean right onto my face. I must have sat there for a long time trying to recover from my frightening experience. I was jarred to reality when a voice behind me said, "Son it is time for us to go back. We must hurry and get on the bus with the rest of the children."

The rest of the children were what I feared the most. I didn't want them to look at me like I was a freak and to make fun of me. The priest said that the children understood. I said to myself, *What do they understand? How to laugh and make fun of somebody who is crippled since infancy by a disease and cannot walk straight? They may laugh and make fun of me now, but I know that my father has faith in God and is following God's plan. I know that my father knows and believes that someday I will be able to walk straight like the rest of the people.*

As I hobbled toward the bus with the tall priest holding my hand, I tried to keep up but couldn't. The priest was so tall that one of his steps equaled three of mine. Besides, I was so weak and nervous from the incident, I hardly had enough energy to walk. Every time the priest would take a step, I tried to keep pace, but my leg would buckle under me, and I would end up on the ground. I tried several times to keep up but could not. I would end up on the ground, being dragged along as if against my will. The priest, out of shear desperation, pity, and frustration, picked me up and carried me onto the bus. The priest certainly was not very happy. He had a disappointed, disgusted look on his face as he pushed me onto the bus. I believe it was after I was on the bus that the priest finally realized what it meant to have two good, strong legs and to be able to walk straight.

Leaving the beach in the late afternoon and riding to the refugee camp took some time. I made my way to our tent where I found everybody ready to eat supper. I joined the family. Father prayed as usual, and we sat down on the floor around the food, which was in the center of the tent. We sat around and waited for mother to pass a small

205

amount of food to each person. My parents were very careful not to waste anything. We ate what we were given and had nothing left over at the end of the day.

After supper, Father said that he had been invited to the Russian Baptist Church where he had met some very fine Christians. That evening, some of the church members came to visit us. Our parents tried to offer them a place to sit, but we had nothing except our sleeping cots, boxes, and the floor in the tent. The people understood the situation and were very friendly and receptive. They invited us to go to their church on Sundays. My parents eagerly agreed.

We were very happy in that church. They had classes for children and adults every Sunday morning. A choir was started in our church, but they told us kids that we were too young to sing in the choir. They also started a small orchestra with some guitars, violins, trumpets, and other band instruments. We wanted to play in the band as well, but the band director said we were too young and didn't know how to read music, but when we got a little older, they would teach us how to read music, and he would allow us to join the church orchestra.

Here is a photo taken in 1954, of the Russian Baptist Church's band in West Sacramento (Bryte) California. Similar Band Nadine Babkina played the trumpet in Shanghai in 1946. The only member of the band still living today is Nidia Babkina, who played trumpet in Shanghai Church in 1946.

25. Photo taken in 1954, in Bryte California of Russian Baptist Church band. Similar Band Nadine Babkina played the trumpet in Shanghai in 1946.

26. Nadine in a more current photo at the age of 100. With her is Mrs. Vera Chenovaya, who traveled with us on the ship from Shangai to America.

Several months had passed since Father had prayed that if it was God's will for us to go to America, He would make it possible for us to go. The rumors had spread throughout the refugee camp and the Russian church that my father was planning to go to America. Of course by now, it was a big joke. Everybody laughed at us, saying that this man was crazy for even thinking of going to America because he and his wife had seven small children, had no money, couldn't speak English, and had no friends in America. We didn't even have anyone to sponsor us to go to America!

They said we had just crawled out of the Gobi Desert like a bunch of desert rats coming out of a rat hole. We had come directly into the refugee camp with nothing on our backs except for torn, worn-out clothes, which were infested with fleas and lice! Now, we wanted to go to America. What a joke!

Everybody in the refugee camp looked at our family and thought we were crazy for thinking of going to America. All the people in the refugee camp wanted to go to America. But how would they get there? Everybody in the refugee camp was poor. They had fled from communism, leaving all of their possessions and wealth behind. All of them had barely escaped with their lives. Many of them had lost their family members, who had been killed. Many of us had lost friends, who had also been killed. Now, all of us were looking for a new country where we could have a home and freedom to worship God.

Even now in Shanghai, the communists were checking everybody. They were especially looking for Russian people with Russian documents and citizenship. The communists would round these people up, put them on trains and ships, and take them back to Russia. As all these people boarded the ships bound for Russia, they were immediately stripped of all their valuables such as jewelry, gold, money, fur coats, and anything else of value. In exchange, they were given plain, old, gray clothes to wear.

Once they boarded the ship and saw the deplorable conditions and how all the people were being mistreated, they had a different picture of the communist utopia in Russia. Many other passengers could not tolerate the drastic change and committed suicide on the ship or jumped overboard and drowned. One young couple were athletes, who were very strong swimmers. After seeing the deplorable conditions on the ship and knowing the fate that awaited them in Russia, they jumped overboard and swam to shore. This couple told us the story of the deplorable conditions on the ships and the conditions that awaited all those who were heading to Russia.

Now it is understandable why God had placed a strong urgency in my father's heart. The urgency was to finish the journey that God had laid out before him as quickly as possible. My father knew that the window of opportunity to escape from communist-controlled areas was closing rapidly on all fronts. This is why Father was always in a hurry to leave.

As in the past, Father was questioned about the destination of the journey. His answer always was, "I don't know. But I know that God knows and wants us to continue our journey." The end of our journey never was revealed to my father, but God planted, in my father's heart, a strong urge and a desire to go forward and to not delay.

Father foresaw the journey in front of him and his family. All the obstacles, such as disease, hunger, cold, danger, and the threat of imprisonment and death, were just human obstacles. They were placed before him and his family by Satan to hinder their journey. Father's goals were set by God. They were far above and beyond the human obstacles. These human obstacles were nothing more than Satan's plan to try to divert and derail God's plan.

God selected his chosen servants, believers, and nonbelievers, and placed them along the journey to guide my father and his family through trials and tribulations to their eventual destination, which was only known to God. The American missionaries in Shanghai sympathized with the sufferings of the stateless Russian Christians and aided Pastor Shelohvostoff, my father, in his goal to reach the United States as soon as possible.

When we heard news about the communists deporting Russians, Father got the family together after supper and once again prayed for safety and deliverance wherever God wanted us to go. Doing God's will was the most important thing in Father's prayers. Father prayed again and said, "If it's Your will for us to go to America, show us the way to get there. Show us the end of our journey and the place where You want us to worship You. Show us the end of the journey where we can live, raise our children, and praise and thank God for His son, who came and gave us eternal life through His death and resurrection."

For the next several months, life in the refugee camp went on as usual. We got used to living in a tent. It was not very difficult for us to learn how to sleep under warm blankets and not to wake up half frozen like we had in the Gobi Desert. While walking across the desert, we had never had three meals a day. We had been fortunate to get some crackers or flatbread with water, and this had not happened every day. Here in the refugee camp in Shanghai we were getting three meals a day, which we had never had before. We thanked God for all the wonderful blessings that He had given us during the entire journey. I knew Father's strong faith in God was the reason that we were here in Shanghai.

27. Photo of Shelohvostoff (Amegin) family in Shanghai in 1947

We continued studying Russian and some English in our classes. Some of the children, including myself, were 100 percent illiterate. We could not read or write in any language. First, they taught us the Russian alphabet. Then they showed us how to read and to write. I remember returning home to my bunk bed and learning the Russian alphabet—how to form the letters on paper. This was a very slow and tedious process, but it had to be done. The teachers were very strict with us. They assigned homework, and it had to be completed by the next day with no exceptions.

We enjoyed going to church on Sundays. The sermons were not very interesting to me because they were over my head, and I didn't quite understand them. However, the music was beautiful. The choir performed every Sunday, as did the orchestra. Sometimes the orchestra would perform with the choir and sometimes without the choir. Either way, the music was very beautiful, and I enjoyed it. I could not wait until I was old enough to be in the choir or in the orchestra.

The Sunday school classes were also very interesting. We talked about the Bible, God, and His Son. I enjoyed them, but I preferred to hear the choir and the orchestra. Most of all I could hardly wait to be old enough to join the orchestra and the choir.

My parents enjoyed going to the Russian Baptist Church. Many times, Father was asked to preach. My father's desire was always to fulfill God's will in life by preaching God's Word to all the people.

Chapter 48

A Ticket to the Land of
Milk and Honey

One day Father received a letter written in English. He could not read English, so he looked at it and put it in his pocket. He carried it in his pocket for several weeks, not knowing what to do with it. He thought about throwing it away, but curiosity got the best of him. He said to himself, *I will find somebody who reads and understands English. I will ask that person to explain to me what is in this letter.* Several weeks went by and father forgot about the letter in his pocket.

One day as he was walking down the street, he happened to reach into his pocket and realized that he still had that letter. He looked at it again curiously and thought, *Well, I have had this for all these weeks, and I don't know what it is. Probably not important, so I will just throw it into this trash can right here.* He extended his arm to drop the letter into the trash can on the sidewalk. Just before dropping it into the trash can, he glanced up. One of the church members was coming toward him from the opposite direction. Father said to himself, *Maybe this brother knows English. Maybe he can read this letter and tell me what it says and what I need to do with it. Should I keep it or throw it away?*

Father held onto the letter as the man approached him. Father asked him, "Brother, do you speak English?"

"Yes," the man replied.

"Do you also read and write in English?"

He answered, "Yes. I teach English to the Russian people. My English is as fluent as your Russian."

Father said, "Would you be kind enough to read this letter and tell me what it says? Should I just throw the letter away or do I need to save it?"

The man read the letter and with great excitement, told my father that it was a letter from American President Lines, a shipping company in Shanghai. He exclaimed, "The letter states that your passage to America has been paid for! You and your family may board the ship any time you are ready to go to America!"

The man was so excited that he had to read it a second time to make sure he had translated it correctly. He again turned to my father and said, "Yes. There is no mistake about it. This is a letter of invitation for you and your family to board the ship to go to America anytime you're ready to go. The ship will take you from Shanghai directly to San Francisco, California. In San Francisco, the Russian Baptist Church will assist you to your final destination in Bryte, California, where you will be the pastor of a small Russian Baptist church."

Father cried out with joy, "Yes! This is the answer to our prayer! God finally revealed to us the final destination of our journey. He also revealed to us the place where He wants me to minister to the people and proclaim His great name!"

AMERICAN PRESIDENT LINES

Trans-Pacific Service • Round-World Service

Shanghai, December 15, 1947

LPO-2788
P-11-S

Mr. Peter Shelokvastaff
209 Yuen Ming Yuen Road, Room 704
Shanghai

Dear Mr. Shelokvastaff:

    We have pleasure in informing you that we
are just in receipt of radio instructions from our
San Francisco Office to furnish you and your family
with prepaid transportation to the value of US$850.00
from Shanghai to San Francisco.

    We understand that you and your family wish to
sail from Shanghai on our SS "~~MARINE SWALLOW~~" Voy-9-E *Gen Meip*
on January 15, 1948 for San Francisco via Yokohama, *Jan 3.*
and we shall be pleased to reserve accommodations for
you upon confirmation that same will be acceptable, by
return mail. Otherwise, we shall be able to offer your
family reservations on the SS "~~GENERAL GORDON~~" Voy-9,
scheduled to sail from Shanghai on January 18, 1948, and
await your instructions as to which of these two sailings
would be most suitable to your travel plans.

    Enclosed herewith is a copy of our information
circular covering our troop transports and we would
request you to read same carefully, completing all the
requirements listed therein, as soon as possible.

    Awaiting your early call at this office to discuss
your travel plans, we remain,

           Very truly yours,

           E. S. Wise
      District Passenger Agent

AChelmis

Enc.

28. Letter Father carried around for two weeks about to throw it away.
Because he did not understand English.

Father thanked the brother, turned around, and hurriedly went back to the refugee camp to tell the good news to his wife and to the rest of the family. By the time Father got to the refugee camp, it was late afternoon. Mother was in the tent while the rest of the kids wandered around the camp.

Father quickly rounded up all the children and brought them into the tent. He showed the letter to us, even though none of us could read English. He said that one of the members from the church had translated the letter, and this man had told him the letter stated that our way to America has been paid for. "This is a letter from American President Lines. In the letter, they told me that our family's passage has been paid for and that we may come aboard and go to America anytime we are ready to go!"

Father immediately prayed and thanked God for answering our prayers. Father said, "We traveled a long way, and we always prayed that God would guide us and protect us on our long journey. I first heard about America from Brother Kazakoff, who was a very powerful witness for God. After I accepted Christ as my personal Savior, I met Brother Kazakoff. Brother Kazakoff and I traveled and preached in many villages across southern Siberia. One time, we were captured by the communists, and while we were trying to escape, Mr. Kazakoff was shot and killed. I escaped.

He told me one time that something bad was going to happen to this country. He said he feared for his family, therefore, he sent his family away to America. He had friends in America. America was a good place to raise a family and live without being persecuted. But there in Russia we could not speak about America. The communists immediately would arrest you and put you in prison for being a traitor, an enemy of the state. Your execution would be immediate. There would be no trial, no hearing, just an execution. The unjust justice would be very swift and deadly.

For that reason all the people were in a pseudo-euphoric mood and always talked upbeat about how great communism was. Communism was building a utopia for all mankind. According to the communists, the whole world was waiting for the inevitable utopia."

However, Father was quite aware of the communist's tactics and methods. For the communists there was only one way—it was the communist way or no way. For that reason, the word *America* was never in my father's vocabulary. He feared that if somebody heard him mention the word "America," the wrong people would hear it, and he would be placed in prison as a traitor and would eventually be executed.

Brother Kazakoff had been very wealthy and had been able afford to send his family to America. All Father could do, at the time, was pray and thank God for the wonderful opportunity of serving Him.

The word "America" had never been spoken since we left Russia. Father feared that the wrong people would overhear it and cause him to be imprisoned for life in Siberian labor camps or be executed. Therefore, he had never mentioned America to any of us until now in Shanghai in the refugee camp.

In our prayers while in the refugee camp, Father prayed about going to America. Even here, the word spread like wildfire that our family with seven children, two adults, no money, no friends, and an inability to speak the language, was planning to go to America. People thought my father was insane to even think of going to America. We became the laughingstock of the refugee camp until God intervened. Then everything changed. *God made the impossible possible!*

Some people in Shanghai and in the refugee camp had been waiting for years to go to America. All these people had money and friends with connections in America and were fluent in multiple languages. All of these people, with the help of their connections, knowledge, and wealth, were still in Shanghai waiting to go to America, while this poor family of nine people, being in Shanghai for less than a year, were getting ready to go to America. How was this possible? From the very beginning of their journey from Russia, they were predestined to go to America as per God's plan.

29. Photo of Amegin family all dressed up and
ready to board the ship—America bound!

30. Photo of receipt from American President
Lines for Lubov Shelohvostoff

Ministers at the Russian Baptist Church in Shanghai had also received word from San Francisco stating that there was a small Russian church in Bryte, California, (now a suburb of West Sacramento) in need of a Russian minister. So the small church in Bryte, California, with the help of Hillside Baptist Church in San Francisco and other individuals, sponsored our family to come to America. The church only consisted of about forty members, mostly old retired Russian refugees. They had no money. The church borrowed the money, and the Shelohvostoff family repaid the money in three years' time, to everybody's surprise.

The church members spoke very little English but were very devout Christian believers, who prayed daily. They prayed for God's wisdom and guidance in selecting the right minister to lead their small congregation. They also prayed that God would remove the Iron Curtain, free God's people, and open the way for God's Word to be proclaimed freely in Russia and the rest of the world. Devout Christian believers worldwide prayed for almost fifty years before God answered their prayer!

God selected and sent a man from Russia, halfway around the world, to fill the empty pulpit in Bryte, California, simply because people prayed earnestly and God heard and answered their prayer.

God heard and answered their prayers, once again, when He appointed a man to go and tell Mr. Gorbachev to tear down this wall. President Reagan, against the advice of all of his immediate staff and the strong advice of his top advisor, told Mr. Gorbachev to "Tear down this wall!" (June 12, 1987). About two years later, the wall came down, and God's Word started to make its way more freely behind the now shattered Iron Curtain. Once again, the impossible became possible!

Photo taken in 1948

Same church building in 2016

31. Letterhead of the church with Father as the pastor and family standing in front of the church that sponsored us

Father and Mother went to night school, learned English, passed their exams, and became US citizens in 1955, at which time we changed our name from Shelohvostoff to Amegin. The family pondered the name change for days and finally came up with Amegin from the Greek words alpha and omega in the Bible. The family liked the name, so we changed it. People could not pronounce or spell our old name. Besides, Father didn't know what they meant when they asked him to spell it!

We boarded the American President Lines ship in Shanghai, China, and sailed out of Shanghai Harbor on January 3, 1948, leaving Tava behind. After our departure from Shanghai, and going to Japan for several days to load and unload passengers and goods, we continued our journey to America, the land of milk and honey. Our destination in America was San Francisco, California.

Tava had to stay in Shanghai for one year by herself after the family left for America. According to the immigration law, Tava, who was eighteen years old, was too old to travel under my parents' documents but was too young to travel by herself. Therefore, by law, Tava had to stay in Shanghai for one year by herself. It was very difficult for her. She was a stranger in a strange land, all by herself, unable to speak the language.

Upon our arrival at the small Russian Baptist church, on the corner of Solano Street and Lisbon Avenue, Brother Chipurenko was the interim pastor (the lay minister who was leading the church). He was one of the church members but later transferred membership to Fresno, California, where he continued to do God's work.

This little church that sponsored us had no parsonage. There were six of us in the family, so Father, Tony, Benny, and some of the church members quickly got together and added a couple of rooms and indoor bathroom onto the back part of the church building. The indoor bathroom replaced the old outdoor toilet in the back of the lot.

Now we had two rooms, a kitchen, and a bathroom with a bathtub. Our indoor toilet was also the toilet used by the congregation during church services. This was incredible: an indoor toilet and indoor hot and cold running water. This was all like a dream. One only dreamed of these things where we came from! This was a dream come true. Father said that it would be enough room for us to live in for the time being, and the church agreed.

After completing the project of adding two rooms to the back of the church building, the church members, who helped build the two rooms, were now in the new room with the family. Father said, "Let us pray and thank God for this wonderful opportunity He has granted us for completing this project, and thank God for this wonderful little church that accepted us and helped us to come to America

For the next several months, we tried to settle down in our new church, our new home, and our new community. All the younger kids went to school. Tony had to work.

Chapter 49

The Last Free Ship Sailing out of Communist Shanghai Harbor

Meanwhile back in Shanghai, Miss Lila Watson, a Southern Baptist missionary working in Shanghai, took Tava under her wing. She found a room for her to live in, in the Russian Baptist church in Shanghai. She found work for Tava washing, ironing, and mending other people's clothes and housecleaning. Tava continued to work hard all the time she was in Shanghai.

Miss Watson also prepared Tava to come to America by teaching her the English alphabet, how read and write English, and about American customs. Tava would work hard all day and then come home and study the lessons that Miss Watson had assigned her. Tava was a hard worker and wanted to know and learn English before coming to America. This went on for a year.

The time for departure from China approached rapidly. Tava went about her work, thinking that she had at least two more weeks to work before she would leave to go to America. The past several days, Shanghai had started changing rapidly. People were running around, rushing from place to place. Many stores were closing down, and she didn't quite understand what was going on. She knew something was not right. Going back to her room after work, she went about her daily routine before retiring for the night.

Shortly before midnight, Tava heard a very loud rapping on her door. "Tava, Tava, get up. We must leave Shanghai right away!"

Tava quickly jumped out of bed, rushed to the door, and found Miss Lila Watson, Reverend Taylor, and Dr. Baker James Cauthen, executive secretary of the Southern Baptist Foreign Mission Board of America, standing there. Miss Watson explained to Tava that the communists had closed all roads and had stopped all boats from leaving Shanghai. "They did not keep their word. Supposedly we had two more weeks before they would slowly start closing all exits. But they lied as usual. We must hurry and get you on the last free ship leaving Shanghai Harbor! The USS General Gordon."

32. Photo of USS General Gordon, the last ship to leave free China from Shanghai Harbor before communists closed all exits from China. Tava's first and last chance to flee communist China!

Tava did not have time to pack any clothes. She dressed, grabbed an overcoat, and walked briskly with her three escorts to an old vehicle, which transported them to the harbor area. As they got out of the vehicle, there was a mob at the dock. People were running, screaming, and dragging their belongings with them. They all wanted to get on the ship.

Armed military guards were everywhere with red bandanas on their arms. The guards were using their guns and bayonets to control the angry mob. The soldiers pushed all the confused screaming people away from the ship. They were trying to restore order!

Finally, after battling the frenzied, screaming crowd of people in front of them, they reached the gangplank of the ship. At least six armed soldiers stood there, keeping everybody back from the gangplank. Dr. Baker James Cauthen, who was dressed in a suit and tie, approached the soldiers very carefully, showing them Tava's papers. A soldier quickly took the papers from Dr. Cauthen, while glancing at them. He rapidly scanned Tava's documents and then carefully focused his attention on Tava. The soldier wanted to be sure of her identity before allowing her to board the ship. He went to the other soldiers and showed them the documents. They all looked at them and looked at Tava. Apparently, they all agreed that the girl standing in front of them was indeed Tava.

Reluctantly, they allowed Miss Watson to escort Tava onto the ship but did not allow the other two to go up the gangplank. In the meantime, the soldiers at the bottom of the gangplank kept a very close eye on Dr. Cauthen and Reverend Taylor. After assuring that Tava was in the hands of the proper authorities on the ship, Miss Watson joined Dr. Cauthen and Reverend Taylor at the bottom of the gangplank. The soldiers, watching Miss Watson as she joined the group on the dock, quickly motioned with their guns for them not to stand around but to keep on moving away from the docks.

The three quickly made their way through the confused and frenzied crowd attempting to get on the ship. They were expecting this type of a situation but not this soon. They thought they had at least two more weeks before the communists started closing all the exits out of Shanghai. Now they had to go back to their hotel and modify all their plans.

Tava left Shanghai on the last free ship (The USS General Gordon) that sailed out of the now communist-occupied Shanghai Harbor.

Miss Lila Watson wrote a book titled *Five Brothers in Four Countries*. In it she states, "Pastor Shelohvostoff (Amegin) had perspective based on retrospection. More definitely than any of the American missionaries, he foresaw the spread of the Communist regime in Shanghai and all over China."[1]

My father and our family, until a year prior to reaching Shanghai, China, were the laughingstock of Kuldja, China. He was considered crazy for even thinking of leaving Kuldja in the midst of a revolution. This was sheer insanity. He must have had a death wish. This man intended to take his eight children, seven of them walking behind the cart. One of the children, an eight year old, who was crippled with polio, hobbled behind the other children, dragging his paralyzed leg while trying to keep up. The man's wife, who was riding the cart, was holding the eighth child, the infant, in her arms, as they crossed China and the Gobi Desert in a homemade two-wheeled cart. The cart was basically big enough only for their belongings and his wife with the infant in her arms. Father was up front leading the old horses. The rest of the family was always walking behind the cart.

Who in his right mind would think he could survive in the Gobi Desert with two old sick horses and seven children walking? People don't travel on old sick horses or walk across the Gobi Desert. The Gobi Desert is for camels. People traveling on horses die in the Gobi Desert. People traveling with camels in the Gobi live. Camels are the best mode of transportation in the Gobi Desert. Everybody knows that. What was this man thinking? Yes, what was this man thinking?

It was very simple, he was not thinking at all. He was only a servant of God, following God's plan. God set the course and the destination. Then God placed a compass in his heart, which was a burning desire, turned him loose in the wilderness, and told him to find his way to the predetermined location chosen by Him.

When we left Kuldja, Sinkiang Province, China, in the middle of the night and in the midst of a revolution, everybody considered us dead. They said that we probably died on the outskirts of town because of the heavy fighting throughout the region. We were quickly forgotten.

They said, "If they survived the heavy fighting and were able to make it out alive, they probably died in the Gobi Desert. They could not survive in the Gobi Desert with eight little children, two old sick horses, and without adequate supplies. How could he have survived with eight small children, a two-wheeled cart, and two old horses walking across the Gobi Desert?"

God showed us the way, and we subsequently reached Shanghai, China. This was all the way from the northwestern Russian Chinese border, across portions of the Silk Road in the Gobi Desert, across the remaining continent of China, and down to the coastal city of Shanghai.

One year later, word reached Kuldja, to everybody's amazement and disbelief, that we were still alive and had reached Shanghai, China. My father and his family fled from communism through the southern Siberian province of Russia, Southern Russia, China, and portions of the Gobi Desert walking.

They eventually arrived in Bryte, California, a small suburb of West Sacramento, California, which was a destination that had been set by God when they were halfway around the world. The only guiding source or clue to this destination was the burning desire to keep going forward on their journey.

When they arrived in Bryte, California, Father said that he knew that this was the end of our long journey. This was the place God wanted him to live. He said that he had no more dreams or strong desires to keep on traveling like he had before. He said he felt peace and happiness in his heart after arriving and settling in Bryte, California.

Chapter 50

Arriving in San Francisco, California

Upon our arrival in San Francisco, Brother Edward Niedens, the main person who helped us and all the other refugees coming to America, met us at the docks. I was at the front of our family as we got off the ship. Every time I would take a step, my left leg would buckle, and I would almost fall to the ground. That didn't stop me from making my way off the ship and onto the ground of our new home. I kept hobbling along with my knee doubling under me every time I walked. Without saying anything to us, Brother Niedens, through his contacts in San Francisco, immediately contacted the Shriners Hospital.

After staying two weeks in San Francisco, we went to our final destination in Bryte, California. In the meantime, Brother Niedens's contacts at Shriners Hospital agreed to take my case at the children's hospital on Nineteenth Avenue in San Francisco.

I was immediately admitted to the hospital and was placed in a room. Shortly thereafter, I was examined by many nurses and doctors and was placed on the surgery schedule for the next day. Throughout the rest of the day and way into the night, the nurses and doctors kept coming into my room to check on me.

I had surgery on my left leg the next morning. When I came out of surgery, I noticed that I had a cast on my left leg, from my hip all the way down to my toes. I found out after surgery that they made two incisions on my left knee, one on one side of the knee and the second on the other side. They made two incisions on my left ankle as well. My leg looked straight after surgery even with the cast on. Wow!

Father was right all along. Even in Kuldja, Father had kept saying that God would lead us to the right people that would help to straighten my leg so I could walk again. He had always refused to give me crutches, saying that the leg would not grow if I used crutches. I remember the heated explosive arguments that they used to have at our house in Kuldja. Men would come over to our house and tell father not to let his son crawl around like a dog on his hands and one good leg. "Your son needs to get a pair of crutches and walk straight like a man!"

Father would answer, "No. He needs to keep using his leg. With crutches he will not use his leg and it will dry up and be lifeless." I remember that Father had always stood his ground and had never given in.

The cast was on my leg for two weeks. I was allowed to sit up in bed, move around, and get into a wheelchair with the help of the nurses. My activities in a wheelchair were limited to the ward on my floor only.

Finally, after two weeks, the doctors removed the cast. They also removed all my sutures. For the next four weeks, the nurses came in twice a day and exercised my leg. They took my leg through all the ranges of motion. I wanted to help move my leg but couldn't because it was paralyzed.

When all the scars had healed, I was taken to a swimming pool where they continued to exercise my leg and put it through the ranges of motion in the water. Initially, my range of motion was very limited, but each week, it got more and more aggressive. They always asked me if I had any pain when they were exercising my leg. I told them I had no pain. The nurses said that was a very good sign.

Several days later, a nurse came in and said, "George, it is time for you to start walking!" That frightened me. Instantly, I had flashbacks of the time when I had walked by placing my hand on my left knee and had drug my leg around. Everybody had looked at me and had made fun of me. They had said, "Look at that cripple. He cannot walk straight. He has to bend down and drag his leg in order to walk halfway straight." Occasionally while walking, my hand had slipped off my knee, and I had fallen on the ground. Then I had gotten up and had tried to walk straight again. It had been very difficult, but I had done it. At times, it had been easier for me to just get on the ground and run like a dog with my two arms and my good leg. I had gotten around much faster that way and had had no pain.

A nurse now helped me out of bed and stood me up. Many doctors and nurses were there. They wanted to see if I would take my first step or fall down. One of the nurses bent down and whispered into my ear, "George, you can take the first step. The doctor fixed your leg so now you can walk straight. Look at the doctor in front of you. He wants you to come to him."

One doctor was several feet away, directly in front of me. I looked at all the doctors and nurses lined up beside him watching me. They were all smiling and happy. My previous horrible experience of falling every time I tried to walk flashed through my mind again. Everyone had thought that had been funny. People had laughed at me. Those horrible memories came back to me at this moment when I needed a clear mind to think with. I thought, *What if I fall down like I did before and they laugh at me? I cannot do this. This is too much for me!*

The nurse continued to encourage me with a soft, gentle voice. Then the doctor who was standing in front of me finally said, "George, come to me," in a tender voice. He urged, "Look at me and take only one step. I know that you can do it. Now place your operated leg in front of you."

At this moment, I had an irresistible urge to reach down and grab my left knee with my left hand just in case I was going to fall. With my left hand on my left knee, I knew I could walk. The doctor anticipated my move and said, "No. Don't touch your leg with your hand. Your leg is fixed. You don't need to hold it any longer. Now put your left leg forward and put some weight on it like you're going to walk on it. Very good. Now place your other leg in front of this leg. Very good."

I did it! I walked without falling down and without holding my leg with my hand! Wow, I could walk! I was overwhelmed with joy. Now I could walk. Just as Father had said, God had sent people to fix my leg. It was a very frightening and very emotional moment for me. The soft voice of the nurse and the doctor looking at me with a smile had a very profound and lasting effect on me.

They continued to encourage me as I began to take more steps without holding onto my leg with my hand. These new images of smiling faces and happy voices overwhelmed my previous horrible images of falling down while everybody laughed at me. The doctors and nurses kept on encouraging me to take more steps and to not be afraid. They gave me strength and courage to walk slowly on a daily basis.

That was the first big hurdle that I had to overcome. From then on, it was more physical therapy, and eventually, I was fitted with a brace that went from my hip down to my ankle. I continue to receive physical therapy while I was in the hospital. After I was discharged from the hospital, the physical therapy nurse came to Bryte to help me. She continued to come for my therapy until she saw that I was doing well.

I used my brace for one to two years. By then, I was strong enough to walk and ride a bicycle without the brace. I had a limp because my left leg was shorter than my right leg, but that did not keep me from participating in physical activities and sports in school as I continued my education.

Chapter 51

Visitation

Father didn't waste any time. Even though he didn't have a car and didn't know how to drive, he started visiting all the Russian people in the area. After learning English by going to night school, he finally got his driver's license. He began to include the surrounding towns. Visitation gradually expanded to San Francisco, Fresno, Bakersfield, and as far as Los Angeles, which was four hundred miles away.

I went with my father on many of the visitation trips to Los Angeles, as well as to other places. He was overwhelmed with the amount of spiritual work that needed to be done. He wanted to proclaim the Gospel of Christ to all the people. He did not go to socialize. He went to discuss the Bible and the plan of salvation.

An example of one of his visitation trips was as follows: One time we drove eight hours to Los Angeles from Sacramento to visit a Jewish family. We stayed two hours, discussed the Bible, discussed the plan of salvation, prayed, and drove the eight hours back to Sacramento. This was typical of my father's visitation plan. Many times people would offer tea or coffee with some type of sweet bread or sour bread with butter, cheese, and salami. Occasionally it would be a full meal. He never asked the church for gas money or spending money for food. He knew the church was very poor and had no money.

As was common in those days, the minister did not receive any type of salary, stipend, or gas money. In gratitude to God for bringing him and his family halfway around the world from Russia to America, Father made a vow to God to preach the Gospel for the rest of his life without accepting a stipend. Father continued to visit all the Russian-speaking people he was able to contact.

One day after the close of the Sunday morning worship service, there was a business meeting. This was held immediately after the closing prayer. Everybody was asked to sit down and not leave. The usual business was discussed and eventually everything was approved.

Then one church member stood up and said, "Brother Shelohvostoff is doing visitation in this area, in San Francisco, in Fresno, in Bakersfield, and as far away as Los Angeles, which is about four hundred miles away. We need to pay him at least gas money for all this traveling and the visitation he is doing on behalf of the church."

There was total silence. The silence was deafening. One could hear a pin drop. Then one brave soul stood up and said in a loud voice, "We did not ask him to do that!"

Again, the silence was deafening. Immediately the subject was changed and the meeting continued with business as usual. Most of the members were past retirement age and were refugees with no income. The majority, if not all of them, were uneducated in the area of tithing and giving. So it was not unusual to pass a collection plate in a worship service with fifty or sixty people present and get nothing more than a few pennies, nickels, and dimes. One could hear a clink, clink, clink, as the coins hit the bottom of the empty collection plate.

Yes, people were educated, wealthy, self-centered, and egotistical. God allowed their hearts to be hardened. They felt independently healthy, wealthy, and strong. They had good health, jobs, homes, and financial resources. God had slowly slipped into second place in their lives.

God, however, was always the center of evening conversation after feasting on a plentiful meal that He had provided. He became a conversation piece, a point of interest, and a point of questionable historical facts—facts that the entire non-believing world had questioned since the fall of man.

Father had lived the financial situation these people were going through. However, it must be pointed out that God brought them out of the desert. He brought them through a war-torn country where disease, starvation, and death lurked at every turn in the road. He brought them through trials and tribulations and into the land of milk and honey. Could they not afford just a little bit more than nickels and dimes in an attempt to try to repay God for the wondrous deeds He had performed by bringing all of them together halfway around the world?

The church in Kuldja had originally started from a handful of believers, who had been organized in 1915–1930 by George Hunter. George Hunter had made frequent visits to the Russian community in Kuldja during his ministry throughout the province of Sinkiang. His ministry in that province had continued until he had been imprisoned in Urumqi by the communists and the Muslims on trumped-up charges. George Hunter, subsequently, had been released from prison and had been banished by the communists and the Muslims from the entire Province of Xinjiang!

Father had continued the church work in Kuldja that George Hunter had started. The group had slowly grown as more Russian people arrived in Kuldja. Eventually it had been organized into a Baptist church. Father had worked in the church as the pastor until we had fled from Kuldja to get away from communist persecution. As the persecution had become unbearable, once again, Pastor Peter Shelohvostoff, his wife Luba, and their eight children, with God at the helm, had spearheaded the venture to flee from communist persecution.

The venture had been in the form of a journey that had begun in the Province of Siberia, had taken them through southern Russia, the northwest corner of China, the Mongolian Gobi Desert, the Silk Road, across the continent of China down to Shanghai, and subsequently to America. This had prepared the way for the rest of his flock to follow their pastor from Kuldja, Xinjiang (Sinkiang), China.

One year after fleeing from Kuldja in the midst of a revolution, everybody had thought that we had either been killed in the fighting while fleeing Kuldja or had died in the Gobi Desert. Then the word had reached Kuldja (now Yining) that the Shelohvostoff family had not only been alive but had survived the war and the walk across the Gobi Desert. They had made it all the way across the continent of China and were now in the coastal city of Shanghai!

The church members had said that if this family could do it with eight children, others could do it too! They had followed their pastor out of the war-torn, communist-controlled Kuldja, Xinjiang (Sinkiang), China, halfway around the world in hopes of coming to the land of milk and honey! But it had been too late! The doors to America had been closed! Even with the help of American missionaries and an immigration attorney, they had still been sent from Shanghai to the Philippines instead of America.

To make the letter stronger and more convincing to those in immigration, the attorney had stated that Pastor Shelohvostoff's family and the church members had traveled together across China from Kuldja to Shanghai. Even this had not helped to bring the group from Shanghai to America. The group had been sent to the Philippines.

Please see the letter that was given to immigration on behalf of the group to assist the group to come to America instead of the Philippines.

December 31, 1947.

Letter of Attorney

From. Group of Russian Baptist Refugees from Singkiang Province.

To.   Reverend Shilohvostov.

    We, group of Russian Baptist refugees, total 55 persons, arrived at Shanghai from Singkiang together with Pastor Shilohvostov.

    We know Rev. Shilohvostov very well, he had been a Reverend of churches in Russia and also in Singkiang, and attends his christian duty so tenderly and pleasantly that we were greatly influenced. Now he is fortunately to have an opportunity to proceed to America and we take this pleasure to authorize him full power to care for us through the Correspondent Mission and the American Government for our emmigration into America. We hope that the American Missions and Russian brotherhood in America will be kind enough to assist him morally and materially and co-operate with him to care of us to emmigrate in the U.S.A.

    Hoping that this request will meet with your approval.

    Thanking you in anticipation.

33. Letter from attorney

Father stated that when he did visitation, he did not think about finances, he only thought about witnessing to all the people who needed Jesus Christ as their personal Savior. He said that made him very happy. This was what he had prayed for all of his life—to be a witness for Christ without being persecuted.

Somehow, he finally felt at peace and had no more urge to keep on going. He felt that God had finally brought him to the end of his journey. He felt that God would always provide in a time of need. As he looked back, he realized that God always provided. Even now, God always provided when he needed help financially, personally, or spiritually. God seemed to know when he needed help and always provided.

Sometimes the help came from the least expected source. This help sometimes came in different forms. Sometimes a person might give him a used tire for his car, which he desperately needed. Other times, somebody else might give or buy him a new tire for his old car. It might be in the form of food, or a brother might say, "Let me fill up your tank with gas. I know that you have a long way to travel and you can use the help."

God provides for us with some of the best things that money cannot buy. Some of these precious needs are physical health, mental health, and spiritual health. If we had poor health, we could not travel, we could not attend church, we could not do visitation, and we could not work and provide for our families. Many times, we all take it for granted that we will always have good health, we will never be sick, and we'll always do what we plan on doing because we are strong! However, God says, "Your life is like a flower; today it is here blooming and beautiful. Tomorrow it will wilt, dry up, and blow away." ISAIAH:40:7 –Paraphrased by Dr. George P. Amegin.

34. Photo of the night bloomers here blooming and
start to wilt when sunlight shines on them.

Such is our life: here today, gone tomorrow. As it is written, "And as it is appointed unto men once to die, but after that the judgment" (Hebrews 9:27). We never know when God will step into our lives and disrupt our best-laid plans!

Suddenly, without warning, you find yourself bedridden and gasping for your last breath of life in this world. You are on the verge of passing on to the other side. However, wait. There are doctors, nurses, friends, families, and ministers, who are all hard at work trying to pull you back into this world. But how can you leave us? Your projects are not complete. What about all the big plans that we made together? Who is going to finish them now? Your mission is not complete. You cannot leave us.

God again intervened and pointed out to man, "There is only one life to live, after which is judgment day. I have set a course for your life and have placed a compass in your heart to guide you. You have followed your course well. You have reached the end of your journey.

"Well done, good and faithful servant. It is time for them to let you go and let me lead you the rest of the way to your new home that I have prepared for you."

Such is life. Always expect the unexpected. Only God knows the past, the present, and the future. For it is written, "Jesus Christ, yesterday, today, and forever the same" (Heb. 13:8).

Father always prayed and thanked God for all the blessings that He had bestowed upon us. God preserved our spiritual, mental, and physical health through the entire journey from Siberia to America. He preserved our spiritual strength and faith through constant prayer throughout the entire journey. Father always prayed that God's will would be done. Father prayed for strength to fulfill His will!

Father continued his church responsibilities, his visitation, his secular job, and started to make arrangements for the group from the Philippines to come to America. There was a total of forty-five individuals. Father immediately realized that would double the size of the congregation in his church. He would have enough people for a large choir, a children's choir, and an orchestra.

With those thoughts in mind, Father continued looking for people to help him sponsor the group of forty-five individuals from the Philippines. He was met with all kinds of excuses. It was too much of a burden. There were too many of them to try and bring to America. We had no resources for the forty-five people. After talking with many Russian Baptist pastors in the area, the general consensus was that it could not be done.

The thought of having a large congregation with a pastor, an assistant pastor, a choir, a children's choir, and an orchestra was overwhelming. He could not think of anything else but that. With those thoughts in mind, he ignored what everybody was saying. He prayed and asked God to help him bring the people from the Philippines to America. He continued praying for wisdom and guidance and that God would send wise and knowledgeable people to help him with this tremendous task with which He had been burdened.

35. Photo of the list of the people in Philippines wanting to come to America. Out of the fifty-five that were on the list, only about forty came. Others went to Australia.

36. Photo of the group in Philippines that wanted to come to America

Father said, "I was their pastor in Kuldja, China, therefore, it is my responsibility to bring the church members together again here in Bryte, California, halfway around the world. Everybody says it is an impossible task, but to God it is a possible task. It is a matter of prayer and faith in God. It usually is a matter of time. With time, God always completes His mission as He planned it."

Brother Edward Niedens was one of the people that helped us to come to America. He again assisted Father by pointing out the right people to talk to, to expedite bringing the group from the Philippines to America. He helped Father in completing the more difficult forms required by customs and immigration. Father did not speak much English. My older sister and I were also very weak in the English language and were unable to help Father do the paperwork.

Brother Niedens, who lived in San Francisco, had a meat market and a Russian deli. Thank God for Brother Niedens, who was always available to help out with the paperwork. Many times, Father would take my older sister, Lydia, or me to help fill out the necessary paperwork properly.

We would go to San Francisco to Brother Niedens's Deli, buy Russian pastry and tea, and sit and enjoy our food. We really enjoyed eating and relaxing while waiting for Brother Niedens to finish his work and come and join us. Brother Edward Niedens would come out and join us for tea and pastry. Then he would help us with the paperwork, which we could not fill out by ourselves.

Edward and Henry Niedens were previous refugees from Russia by way of Shanghai, China, who came to America in 1934. Edward and Henry were a big asset to Father in helping with the documents and all the translation that had to be done in order to get all the legal paperwork completed. They, along with other pastors from several churches, were able to lend support for my father's project to bring the rest of the church members from the Philippines to America.[2]

The local church members and members from other churches were very reluctant to assist Father and sponsor the refugees from the Philippines. Father would explain repeatedly how important it was for them to be here. It would double their congregation, and they could do more things for God. They could have a large choir, orchestra, and Sunday school classes. However, they kept on questioning the idea, "Forty-five people will be sponsored by us? There are only a handful of us here. There are too many of them and too few of us. We have homes, we have responsibilities, and we have families to feed. We have bills to pay. How can a handful of us sponsor such a large group from halfway around the world? It can't be done!"

After visiting the local churches' ministers and getting a negative response from all of them, Father prayed and asked for wisdom and guidance in bringing the church family to America from the Philippines. As always, he listened to the still, small voice within him that told him that it could be done. He proceeded to contact wise, knowledgeable people who were willing to help him with the paperwork and the legal side of preparing all the papers for these people to come to America. This preparation took almost two years. It required my father, my older sister, Lydia, and me to travel about eighty-five miles to San Francisco on a weekly basis to complete the paperwork.

There was also the burden of what it cost to sponsor all these people to come to America. Upon arrival of all of these immigrants from the Philippines to America, it was the responsibility of the sponsor to assure that all of the working members of each sponsored family had a job. This was a big responsibility for my father. My sister Tava and my older brother Tony gave their jobs to the newcomers. One by one, we helped get jobs for all the working family members of the group.

The American Consul and immigration in San Francisco saw how eager, sincere, and determined Father was in trying to help bring these people to America. With compassion and understanding, the Department of Immigration was able to help them with proper documentation and to fill out some of the necessary forms. They knew that Father could not speak English but was determined to go there and do his best to help other people.

Brother Niedens was always available to help as much as he could. He had a business to operate, yet he always found time to sit down in his deli and assist us with the paperwork.

Before long, the entire department of immigration and naturalization in San Francisco knew my father and his goal. They knew that he could not do everything alone because of the language barrier, the financial barrier, and the distance that he had to travel weekly to comply with the requirements. Everybody in the department became so familiar with my father's task and struggle to bring the large group from the Philippines to America, they did as much legal work for him as they could to expedite the paperwork. Even though Lydia, Benny, or I went with Father to help him with the paperwork and translation, we still had language problems. At that time, Benny, Lydia, and I were still struggling with the English language.

After about sixteen months of traveling to San Francisco on a bimonthly or monthly basis, we were exhausted. Finally, the San Francisco immigration office informed us that we were almost done with the paperwork and that it was just a matter of time before all the completed paperwork would be in the hands of the immigration and naturalization people. From that point on, they would proceed and work with the American consulate in the Philippines to bring the group to America.

The immigration and naturalization people told Father that everything had been done. They told him to go back to Bryte (West Sacramento), to wait until they notified him of their progress, and that he did not need to come to San Francisco until further notice. They told him that everything had been completed by him and by the immigration and naturalization office in San Francisco. Now they would have to wait.

The American consulate in the Philippines would need to handle its end of the paperwork now. It would identify each person, take a photograph, and prepare the documents for them to come to America. When the consulate in the Philippines completed its work, it would notify the office in San Francisco, and that office would proceed from there.

In the meantime back in Bryte, preparations were underway to receive this new group of refugees from the Philippines. The good news was that they were all coming to Bryte. Now the small church that Father pastored on Lisbon and Solano also got very excited and pitched in to help in welcoming the new immigrants, assigning them places to stay and jobs, which were already waiting for them upon their arrival.

When they arrived in Bryte, there was a big gathering and a celebration at Pastor Shelohvostoff's house on 733 Solano Street. During the celebration, the head of each family spoke, prayed, and gave gratitude to God for the wonderful reunion of this church in America. This same church existed halfway around the world in China and now was in America. It was a miracle of modern times how God could move all these people halfway around the world and bring them together in Bryte, California. What seemed impossible to everybody was possible to God. Now there they were in the land of milk and honey, praising and thanking God for bringing them together again.

Life in the little church on the corner of Lisbon and Solano continued under the leadership of Pastor Peter Shelohvostoff. As the church grew, a choir was organized. They thought of forming an orchestra, but the lack of instruments and players delayed it. The church did organize a Sunday school, though.

With the growth of the church and the addition of more and more activities, there rose a discontent among the members. Each group wanted to do things its way and not the way the Bible or the pastor wanted it. As a result of this discontent, a small group under the leadership of Pastor Shelohvostoff left the church and started meeting in the VFW Hall three blocks from the church.

37. Photo of the VFW hall where we met

This is where the small group met while the new church was being built on the corner of Solano Street and Hobson Ave. They were ridiculed for meeting in the VFW Hall, which was a bar. Each Sunday morning, all the children of the small group along with some twenty-five adults, such as the Shelohvostoff family, the Johnny Granchukoff family, the Peter Granchukoff family, the Podany family, would come early to pick up all the beer bottles and cigarette butts. They would clean and sweep the hall and get it ready for Sunday school and worship service. This went on for about two years. In the meantime, my brother Tony, who worked in construction along with Johnny and Peter Granchukoff, found two empty lots for sale on the corner of Solano Street and Hobson Avenue in Bryte.

Chapter 52

The Opening of the New Russian Baptist Church in Bryte

In spite of all the ridicule, this small group of believers purchased the corner lot and started to build a small church. Brother Rudneff, a retired artist, and his wife moved their trailer onto the property and maintained the property and the building in exchange for their rent. This new church was located about one block from the original small church that sponsored us to come to America. (See the photo of the new church that was built basically by the Rev. Peter Amegin family, Tony Amegin family, Alex Amegin family, Johnny Granchukoff family, Peter Granchukoff family, Mr. and Mrs. Podany, Vasiliy (Bill) Lokteff, and the Ashanbrenoff family. A few others would come and help when the spirit moved them. This handful of members built this church against many odds and strong opposition.)

We completed the new Russian Baptist Church on the corner of Solano Street and Hobson Avenue in 1952. After the completion of the new addition to the church, under the leadership of Pastor Amegin (Shelohvostoff), a celebration was in order. As you can see in the photo, many visitors, guests, and friends from other churches were there.

38. Photos of the new church in Bryte during the opening celebration

39. Celebration with many people attending

40. Dr. Posey, president of the Southern Baptist
Association of California, congratulating father on
opening the new church in West Sacramento (Bryte).

The church still stands today with a beautiful new larger sanctuary addition to the existing building under the leadership of Reverend Daniel Lokteff. The building today serves as one of the original churches located on the corner of Hobson Avenue and Solano street in West Sacramento (Bryte), California.

Under the leadership of Reverend Peter Shelohvostoff, the new church slowly grew. In the meantime, the original church where my father pastored, one block away from the new church, continued to have its share of problems. The small group that remained there after we left was quite discontent again with their current situation and could not get along with each other; they just could not see eye to eye. The remaining members in the original small church split again, with only a handful of believers in each group. Some of the members from these splintered groups had no place to go. One by one they slowly started drifting into the new church. It was this influx of members from the other splinter groups into our new church that caused discontent among the church members once again.

Around this time the Slavic Churches Association of the West Coast held a convention in Fresno, California. Father planned on going to the Association meeting. As he was leaving, a certain brother came up to my father and said to him, "Dear Brother Amegin, would you be kind enough to deliver this letter to the president of the Association before the meeting starts?" Father said certainly, he would do that. Upon reaching Fresno, Father met with the president of the Association and personally gave him the letter that he was asked to deliver to him. After the Association meeting, Father drove home and continued his church work and his secular job.

During the meeting in Fresno, Father realized that he was getting very cold treatment from most of the people who were at the meeting. In all the previous meetings in the Russian churches in California he was welcomed and appreciated as a new pastor of the Russian Baptist Church in Bryte, California. But now he could not explain why he received such a cold reception from all the leading pastors at the meeting. He did not let that bother him, but continued doing his church work as usual.

It was as if it was not enough that our family had journeyed halfway around the world from Russia to America enduring many hardships such as persecution for their faith, facing death, starvation, disease, and loss of an infant during the journey. The family, in spite of all that, remained faithful to God.

Chapter 53

Satan Tests Father

Now, Satan came to God and said, "Hey, God you made it too easy for this man. He had it made in the shade. You placed your trusted servants from the very beginning of the journey to the end of the journey to guide him. How could he go wrong? The journey was lined with Your trusted servants. They were like a row of lit-up Christmas tree lights. All he had to do was follow the lights from the beginning to the end. Even I could not have made it any easier for him!

But now, Satan said to God, "Let me test him my way and see if he remains faithful to You!" (Book of Job). God allowed Satan to test father's faith

About a month after the meeting in Fresno, we had unusual visitors at our house on Solano Street. These visitors drove a big black car with government tags on it. The two men that got out of the car wore dark suits and ties. They came to the front door and knocked. I was outside playing in the front yard and saw the car pull into our driveway. I saw the two men get out of the car and go to the front door, and heard them knocking. Father answered the door, and they asked him in Russian if his name was Reverend Peter Shelohvostoff. Father replied, "Yes, that's my name; I am Reverend Peter Shelohvostoff."

"May we come in and talk with you?"

Father said, "Yes."

The two men walked into the house and Father closed the door behind them. They talked for two days behind closed doors. Children were not allowed into the room. Many times my mother would leave the room and close the door behind her. She would go back into her bedroom, close the door, and cry. This went on for two days. My parents said nothing to us children about the meeting with these men. The third day started off the same way—Mother would go in the room with Father and the two men, and shortly she would come out crying. She would go to her room in the back and continue crying behind the closed door.

We were getting very concerned; however, we still knew nothing of the matter.

On the third day, after staying only two hours, the two men got in their vehicle and left. No one ever said anything about the meeting to any of us. Then, a month later, my father said he needed to go to Los Angeles to meet with these men that came to our house. He asked me to go with him to keep him awake as he drove the ten-hour trip from Sacramento to Los Angeles. This meant that we had to drive a very old, well-used car with tires that had very little or no tread.

We always purchased our spare tires at a salvage yard. There, the tires were affordable but not always the best. However, the tires that we bought there were always better than the ones on the wheels of the old jalopy that we were driving. We always drove slowly to prevent having a flat tire or a blowout on the road. On long trips such as this one, we always had two spare tires in the trunk and the tools to fix the flats.

The building that we reported to in Los Angeles was a federal building. Father and I went into the tall building. On the first floor of the building, we found the office number. A bench was in front of the office door. Father said to me, "George, you sit here and wait until I come out. Then we will drive back home." I sat there and waited for couple of hours and, finally, Father came out and said, "Okay, now we can go back home to Sacramento." Home, of course, was another ten-hour drive away.

Father and I continued making these trips to Los Angeles for the next three months. He would never make any comments on the nature of the trips to Los Angeles, so, I started thinking maybe they were testing my father to get him ready to become an American citizen. Naturally I got excited, and on the way back to Sacramento I was happy and cheerful. I thought, *Just think, we will become citizens of America very soon.* I could not think of any other reason why we would travel 400 miles to meet with some people in an office for two hours, and then drive 400 miles back to Sacramento.

I asked Father about the next trip to Los Angeles. Father replied, "The man told me that we don't have to come to Los Angeles anymore. They will let us know of the situation. They will tell us what we need to do and when."

Several weeks went by and we heard nothing. Then one day around noon, a black government car pulled up into our driveway again. This time, only one man came out of the car while the other man sat in the car waiting. The man approached the door and knocked, and Father let him in. The man did not stay too long, maybe thirty minutes to an hour, and then he came out of the house, got in his car, and they drove away.

Father feared communists. He was very scared when these men were there, but he would not show it. Father got the family together. We prayed and that is when he explained to us why the two men came to our house. He explained that the men said they had written proof in the form of a letter with about twenty-five signatures from our church members and others in the community here in the Bryte and Sacramento area, accusing my father of having been a communist. Furthermore, my father and his entire family needed to be deported back to Russia immediately without delay.

Now it was clear to us why Father did not inform the children of the situation. This also explained very clearly why our mother kept crying all the time the men were visiting our house. She knew what was going on but would not tell us about it. Father said, "God knew that people would do this; therefore, He made preparations for this moment many years ago." He proceeded to tell us about his friendship with Mr. Kazakoff, and how his friend had been shot by the communists.

"Several days before Mr. Kazakoff was killed by the communists, he said, 'Peter, this country is unstable. I fear something terrible is going to happen in the near future in this country. I started thinking like this a long time ago. Now, I see it unfolding before my eyes. I see nothing but danger, trouble, starvation, and death everywhere in Russia.

"Mr. Kazakoff continued, 'When I first started seeing these visions almost a year ago, I decided to send my family to America where they would be safe. I have friends in Los Angeles who will help my family upon their arrival in America. They will see that my children would get a good education in America.'

"These two federal agents that came to visit us from Los Angeles were the sons of Mr. and Mrs. Kazakoff. I met them in Siberia in their home before they left for America and before their father was killed!

"Mr. Kazakoff, was killed by the communists as the two of us fled for our lives with bullets flying all around us."

I met and spent two weeks with Mr. Kazakoff's family before they left for America. I remember meeting the two little boys. They spoke fluent Russian. They said they remembered me and the stories that their mother told about their father and me.

Father went on. "These two federal agents from Los Angeles did extensive research into my background and concluded that all the allegations against me and our family were false, and that I am not a communist. They said they did not find a shred of evidence against me. They personally wrote letters in our favor to the government, acknowledging the fact that their father and I fought communists together in Russia. So on this last visit, when the older son came here last week, he informed us that we were cleared of all accusations. He assured us that we would not be deported to Russia." He also told my father to make sure to tell his wife, Luba, to stop crying, she was not going to be deported.

In retrospect, the letter that Father was given to deliver to the Association meeting was the letter accusing him of being a communist and needing to be deported. That would explain the cold reception that Father got from many pastors at the convention. If Father was dishonest, he would have opened and read the letter, and may have been able to stop the spread of lies and accusations. The letter was given to my father knowing that he could be trusted not to open it. God anticipated that man would follow his sinful instincts. Therefore, He prepared a better plan that was already in place, a foolproof plan that He prepared before the journey from Russia to America ever began. Father did not need to open the letter to find out what was in it. It was not necessary. God already took care of the problem before the journey was even started in Siberia.

Apparently since the plan backfired, and the Amegin (Shelohvostoff) family did not get deported, there arose more unpleasantness in the church.

Chapter 54

The Beginning of the Russian Baptist Mission in Sacramento

Fruitridge Baptist Church on Fruitridge Boulevard in Sacramento under the leadership of Rev. Bowlinger, allowed the small group of believers to use their facilities until the group purchased a large house on 26th street to start their mission in Sacramento, California.

Since Johnny Granchukoff's family was already living in Sacramento, it was easy for them to start a mission there. Brother Johnny Granchukoff was married to my sister Tava. Johnny, Tava, brother Garin, and others had been carrying on visitation in Sacramento for several years. The small group of believers initially met at Fruitridge Baptist Church in Sacramento. Other believers followed and joined the mission in Sacramento. The group was large enough now that the discussion turned to purchasing a building for the new mission. A large house was purchased on 26th Street. The small group of believers started to meet in their new location. The fellowship continued between the Fruitridge Baptist Church under the leadership of Rev. Bowlinger and the small newly Russian mission.

The newly formed Sacramento Evangelical Russian Baptist Mission was started at 1625 26th Street, in a home.

41. Photo of the house located on 1625 26th St.,
where the Sacramento Mission started

Immediately others joined the mission in Sacramento. Brother Garin, Peter Granchukoff's family, Reverend Peter Amegin's family, Mr. and Mrs. Podany, Tony Amegin's family, and a few others continued to join and do God's work in the Sacramento Evangelical Russian Baptist Mission on 26th Street.

In the meantime, the new church on the corner of Hobson and Solano in Bryte, (now West Sacramento) California grew slowly after the Shelohvostoff family transferred to the Sacramento mission.

Father was invited to become the pastor of this new mission in Sacramento on about the July 1964. (See letter written by my father to my sister telling her that he accepted the position as the pastor of the Franklin Mission in Sacramento, California.) There were about twenty members in the mission and about twenty children attending on Sundays. They liked it!

От папы и мамы
Амегиных, 8/21-64 г.
Брайт Кал.

Дорогим в Господе Лидии и Дэйлу МИР ВАМ ОТ ГОСПОДА!

В первый раз мы с мамой,побыли продолжительно в Парке
Эсимите /11 дней/ и так хорошо Господь подкрепил нас,
через чудную природу и климат,а особенно через воду;
которая очень и очень хорошо помогает,очищая организм.

Ты просила,чтоб ответить тебе,на некоторыя интирисующия
тебя вопросы, которыя иногда тебе требуются.

Вот мы на все твои вопросы отвечаем.

Церковь в которую мы вступили,вновь организованная не боль-
шая, свыше двадцати членов,почти столько-же и детей.
С вступлением в церковь я приня и пресвитерское служение.
Хлопочим о приезде молодого пресвитера из Канады,фамилия
его:Карпиш.По приезду его,я передам ему мое пресвитерское
служение.Но дело с приездом его почему-то замедлилось,но
надеемся на Божие проведение,да будет вовсем Его святая воля.

1.мое рождение:Село------/ЗАКОВРЯШИНО,это название деревни.
2.страна:--Росия,---провинция:---Сибирь.Год рождения:--1897.

42. Photo of letter Father wrote to Lydia and Dale

43. Rev Peter and Luba Shelohvostoff

255

In the meantime, after we left the original little church on the corner of Lisbon and Solano Street that sponsored our family to America, it started to have disagreements in leadership again. As was stated previously, Father and a few members left and continued to meet in a VFW hall several blocks away. The remaining members in that little church were having problems and split the second time. Now there were only seven members left in that original little church on the corner of Lisbon Avenue and Solano Street.

Initially, everything went well in the new church, and then discontent grew again, especially since people thought the Amegin family was to be deported and then they were not. Father continued to pastor that church on the corner of Solano and Hobson in Bryte. There were too many chiefs and not enough Indians; everybody wanted to run the church their way.

The discontent continued, so the group that built the church on the corner of Solano and Hobson once again left the church they built instead of arguing and bickering. As it is stated in the Bible, the harvest is ripe and plentiful, so they went to Sacramento and continued to do God's work by working in a mission there that Johnny and Tava Granchukoff started. They were meeting at the Fruitridge Baptist Church under the leadership of Rev. Kenneth Bowlinger in Sacramento. They were joined by Brother Garin and a few others that lived in that area.

At that time I was attending The Golden Gate Baptist Theological Seminary in Mill Valley, California (San Francisco Bay Area). I was invited on weekends to work with the young people in the mission in Sacramento.

I lived with Rev. Platon Chartschlaa's family in Dom Evanglia on the corner of Balboa and 19th Avenue in San Francisco where Rev. Paul Rogozin was Pastor. Rev. Platon Chartschlaa and family were recent arrivals from Argentina. Their ability to speak and understand English was limited. Brother Platon invited me to live with them, saying the church was three stories high, and the basement had about five or six rooms that were empty. I could choose any room I liked and live there rent free. While doing my studies at the seminary, I helped Platon and his children with their homework in English. It was a great trade-off—I was living with a wonderful Christian family rent free, and was using my English skills to help the family. To economize further, we rode in one car to the seminary.

During the time that the small group was meeting on 1625 26th Street in Sacramento, they started looking for land to build a church on. They had no funds, so they approached Rev. Bowlinger of Fruitridge Baptist Church. They were granted a loan of $25,000 for their project!

They found an empty lot on the corner of Franklin Boulevard and First Avenue. A nightclub that was there had accidently burned down. Now the lot was empty. Johnny and Tony approached the owner with an offer to buy the property. The owner said that they were going to rebuild the nightclub. One of the city officials suggested my father, Tony, and Johnny take a census of the neighborhood, asking the people whether they wanted a nightclub on that spot or a church. The consensus of the neighborhood was that they wanted a church. They did not want a nightclub on that spot. With this information in hand, the owners were approached and were informed of the findings. The owners were asked if they were willing to sell the property to a church, and they agreed to sell it.

At that time a new expressway was being built through Sacramento. Many buildings, new and old, were being scheduled to be demolished or moved to make room for the new expressway. Alex, my younger brother, was working on building the expressway in that area, he found out about a new funeral home that was scheduled to be demolished to make room for the expressway. The sanctuary of this new funeral home would seat about 150 people.

Brother Johnny, Pastor Shelohvostoff, Tony, and Alex approached the city leaders and proposed to buy and move the building at no cost to the city. In fact, the city would make money with this transaction. It would save the city the trouble of paying a company to demolish the building and clear the area of all the debris, and at the same time, the city would make a profit. The city leaders agreed to sell the building to the new future Evangelical Russian Baptist Church to be built on Franklin Boulevard.

This was such a bold and risky move on the part of just a handful of believers. It took a lot of prayer and hard work for the few able-bodied men in the small group of believers. Basically it was Johnny Granchukoff, Peter Granchukoff, Tony Amegin, Alex Amegin, Brother Garin, Brother Dubuk, and a few others who made this bold move to purchase the building and move it to Franklin Boulevard.

First they made the decision to build a basement the size of the structure. This required special tools and machinery that they didn't have. Therefore, they elected to hire out that part of the project to special contractors who had all the necessary equipment for the job. Upon completion of the basement, and moving and placing the ready-made sanctuary on top of the basement, they would instantly create a two-story building. There would be plenty of classrooms for Sunday school. Also there would be a lot of room for a big fellowship hall. So the construction began by digging a basement. Once the hole was premeasured and dug, then the wall and the floor were poured from concrete.

My brother, Alex, who worked in building bridges, expressways, and laying concrete foundations, assisted in assuring that everything was done according to city building codes. Since Alex worked closely with the city inspectors, he helped by inspecting everything before the inspectors would come. He made sure that every phase of the construction was done according to the specified building and city codes. Alex knew the codes better than any of the other church members.

After completion of the building project, the church ended up with a two-story building. This two-story building served two purposes. The lower section, or basement, consisted of a fellowship hall that could accommodate 100-plus people, several Sunday school classrooms, a kitchen, and the restrooms.

44. Photo of Baptistry scene and Artisit E. Garin at Franklin Church

The second floor consisted of a platform across the entire front of the auditorium. Behind the platform was the baptistry. Behind the baptistry was a beautiful lifelike painting covering the entire back part of the baptistry from the floor to the ceiling. The painting consisted of mountains, trees, and a river winding down from the mountains via a small waterfall that ended up in a small peaceful pond-like body of water directly behind the baptistry. A very talented and active church member, Brother Garin, an artist who was known in several continents of the world, created and completed this painting during the time that the main auditorium was completed. We thanked God for such talented people who are great servants of the Almighty God.

45. Photo of Dr. George Peter Amegin Author of this Book

46. Dr. Amegin's Art Work

The front and center part of the platform was for the pulpit. The piano was at the right side of the platform. In the center of the auditorium was the seating section of the building with a center aisle vacant of chairs. The sides also had no chairs. That way people could go from the front to the back of the auditorium by either side or through the center part of the auditorium. The back portion of the auditorium consisted of restrooms on one side of the auditorium. On the other side was a cry room or baby room for mothers with children or infants who were crying and had to be fed. They could take them to the back room and care for the infants. The whole front of the cry room was glass and had speakers, so the mothers there with their infants were able to hear all the sermons and other activities in the church auditorium. Therefore, as one entered the church building, the baby cry room was to the left and the restrooms were on the right side of the entry hallway. The center part continued as the entry hallway into the church.

47. Photo of the original members taken in front of the church
on Franklin Boulevard after the completion of the building

After working for many years for the Southern Pacific Railroad
Company painting the inside of railroad cars with lead spray paint,
my father's health started failing him. At the outset of the building
of this church, he suggested we look for a pastor to take his place. We
heard about Brother Karpiec in Canada who was available, and made
arrangements to bring Reverend Karpiec, Mrs. Karpiec, their daughter,
and her parents from Canada to Sacramento to take over the position
of the pastor.

After the arrival of the Karpiec and their in-laws, a total of five
people, they had no place to live, so they lived with Johnny and Tava
Granchukoff on Fifth Ave., about five blocks from the New Franklin
Church in Sacramento rent free for one year. Subsequently, Brother
Karpiec's family purchased a large house within walking distance of the
church and his family was able to move into their new home.

Upon the arrival of the new pastor from Canada, Father became less
and less active in the church. Previously he would travel all day, work

all night, and travel some more and it wouldn't bother him, but now he required much more rest than before. He continued to do visitation in the Sacramento area. Then his health began failing him rapidly. He stopped his visitation and his preaching.

Brother Johnny Granchukoff, who was married to my sister Tava, continued to grow spiritually. Johnny and Tava moved from Sacramento to Washington State where Johnny Granchukoff was ordained. Johnny and Tava continued to do church work in that region. He became a very powerful witness for Christ. His visitations and prayers with new believers were very powerful and compelling. Brother Johnny and Tava extended their ministry along the West Coast north into Oregon, Washington, and Canada, and even traveled to Australia, where he was asked to stay and continue to do God's work there. Subsequently they moved to Washington, where they continued preaching, teaching, and doing visitation with all the Russian people in that area.

Numerous times Johnny was invited as the guest speaker at American Baptist churches in the area of Washington State and Southwestern Canada. Articles were published in local papers about his preaching, and the testimonies Johnny and Tava, gave.

48. Photo of the Granchukoff family

My father became terminally ill and eventually went to be with the Lord on June 15, 1967.

One of many profound memorable statements that father told us was this: "A rich man has the world at his feet and goes and does as he pleases. The poor man has nothing and goes only where God leads him!"

My father's lifelong desire was to fulfill God's will. Indeed, he fulfilled God's will in his life. He remained faithful until the day God took him! This book is the final chapter in father's lifelong quest of fulfilling God's will in his life! This book also serves as the beginning of the quest for the will of God by the people seeking wisdom, knowledge, understanding and eternal life through our Lord Jesus Christ! The quest begins by accepting Christ as your personal Savior.

For it is written, "I am the way, the truth, and the light: no man cometh unto the Father except through me!" (John 14:6).

THE END

49. Amegin Family Photo

About the Amegin Family Today

Parents: Deceased

Tava: Deceased, leaving six children, grandchildren, and great grandchildren.

Tony: Deceased, leaving four children and grandchildren. Nina, his wife, still living.

Benny: Deceased 1962. While studying for the ministry in Multnomah School of the Bible, Ben and three others wanted to hear Billy Graham preach during his crusade in Fresno, California. In the summer of 1962, Ben and three others flew in a private plane from Sacramento, California, to Fresno, California, to attend a Billy Graham crusade in Fresno. They never returned and were never found, until 30 years later, a hiker in Yosemite Valley, California, found a wreckage of a plane which was identified as the one they were flying. A partially burned identification card was found and identified as one belonging to one of the travelers in the group!

Lydia: Deceased, leaving three children and grandchildren.

Alex: Retired from construction, Donna, his wife, retired from working for the State of California. Alex and Donna are enjoying their children and grandchildren.

Nida: Married to Mike Lokteff. Both are retired from operating the Word to Russia radio program. However, they did not retire from God's service! They have touched many hearts and changed lives of many people through their tireless witnessing and personal interaction with people during their numerous travels to Russia and other parts of the world! Mike and Nida still find time for their children and grandchildren. While they do love traveling, enjoying their children and grandchildren continues to be their priority.

George: After graduating from West Texas State University with a B.S. degree, he received his masters degree from Golden Gate Baptist Theological Seminary in Mill Valley, California (in the San Francisco bay area). He then pursued his studies in medicine. After four years received his doctors degree in osteopathic medicine. He then joined the military where he completed three more years of studies to become an eye surgeon. After 23 years in the military he still is practicing medicine, doing eye surgery, and missionary work in Mexico. Doctor Amegin currently is completing his work towards his doctor of divinity degree!

A Personal Word from George Amegin

Since the passing of my wife, Edith Adrian Porter Amegin on January 18, 2013, I stay busy practicing medicine, performing eye surgery, and doing missionary work! I find time for my kids, grandkids, and great grandkids! Other free time is used in praising God with my trumpet in church! Hobbies--I enjoy gardening, playing, teaching the piano, and oil painting!

Author's Biography

Name: George Peter Amegin, D.O., P, A,

Date of Birth: 9/6/1937

Place of Birth: Kuldja, China

Citizenship: United States of America

Marital Status: (Widower): Wife Edith (Porter) Amegin

Children: Natasha May 15, 1968
                   Daniel October 24, 1969
                   John Marc March 15, 1972
                   Peter Guy May 3, 1973

Languages: Russian (Fluent)
                   English (Fluent)
                   Spanish (Semi-Fluent)
                   German (Understand And Read)

Education: 1956 - 1958 Wayland Baptist University
                   Plainview, Texas
                   1958 - 1961 West Texas State University,
                   Canyon. Texas Major- Biology (Pre-Med)
                   Degree B.S.

Post Graduate: 1962-1965 Golden Gate Baptist Theological
Seminary
Degree - Master in Religious Education
1966 - 1970 University Health Science Center
College of Osteopathic Medicine, Kansas
City, Mo.
Degree- Doctor of Osteopathy

Internship: 1970-1971 Hillcrest Osteopathic Medical Center
Oklahoma City, Oklahoma Rotating

Family Practice: 1971-1975 Oklahoma City, Oklahoma

Military Rank/
Dates: Lieutenant Commander 1976
Major -1978
Lieutentant Colonel 1980

Active Duty
Military: US Navy 1976-1978
US Army 1978-1992

US Army Reserves: March 1992-1999

Board Certification 1971 National Boards - #1606
Febuary 29, 1988 American Osteopathic Board
of Ophthalmology and Otorhinolaryngology
(Written and Oral 1986, Surgical and Clinical
1987)

Licensure: 1971 Kentucky - Inactive
1971 Oklahoma - Inactive #1568
1977 Mississippi - Inactive #7879
1979 California - Inactive #20a4428
1990 Texas - December Current - H8566

Accomplishments: 1976 Navy Undersea Nuclear Medicine,
Washington D.C
1976 Sub Doctor, Groton Submarine Base, Ct
1978 Gulfport Seabee Base, Gulfport, Ms

1981-1984 - Official Speaker In Ophthalmology
For 77th Command, European Physicians
Assistant And Primary Care Of Provider
Refresher Courses.

Special Positions: 1981-1984 Consultant To 15 Outlying Health
Clinics
With Population Of 75,000 Active Duty
Dependants
And Retired Personnel Within A 12,000 Square
Mile Area
To Provide Health Care To Patients
And Continuous Education To General
Medical, Staff
Ophthalmoloists At Erlangen
University - 1982-1984
Instrumental In Organizing And Starting The
Intraocular Lens Implant Program In American
Military Hospitals In West Germany

1981- 1984 Official Speaker In Ophthalmology
For The 77th MEDICAL COMMAND,
EUROPEAN PHYSICIANS ASSISTANT
And Primary Care Provider Refresher Courses

Official Speaker In Ophthalmology For Ambulatory
Patient Care Conference, Garmisch, West Germany

Ophthalmology Consultant To:
Fort Huachuca, AZ. Mescalero Indian Reservation
White Sands Missile Range, Holloman Air Force Base, NM

Teaching Staff, Plastic Surgery Residency Program,
William Beaumont Army Medical Center, Fort Bliss, Texas

1985 -1986 Asst. Chief, Department of Ophthalmology,
William Beaumont Medical Center, Ft. Bliss, Texas

1986-1992 Adjunct Clinical Professor, University of
Houston, College of Optometry, Houston, Texas

1987 - 1990 Assistant Chief under Colonel Raspberry in Department Of Ophthalmology at William Beaumont Army Medical Center where I devoted much time teaching residents, interns, and nursing students

1987 - 1992 Lectured in Ophthalmology Regularly in Emergency Room as well as Troop Clinic, Fort Bliss, Texas

1988 -1992 Clinical Assistant Professor,
Department of Ophthalmology and
Visual Sciences, Texas Tech
University Health Sciences Center School of
Medicine, Lubbock, Texas

1988 -1992 Teaching Staff, Oral, and
Maxillofacial Surgery
Present Residency Program, William Beaumont
Army Medical Center, Fort Bliss, Texas

1990 - 1992 Chief, Department of
Ophthalmology,
William Beaumont Medical Center, Fort Bliss,
Texas
1996-Present
World Health Care Foundation
January 1998 - December 1999 Chief
Department of Surgery, Edinburg Regional
Medical Center, Edinburg, Texas

2016 to Present
Member of the Advisory Board for
The College of Health Care Professions
Mcallen, Texas

2015 to Present Member, Board of Directors for
Edinburg Theological Seminary

Private Practice : General Ophthalmology
March 1, 1992 - Present

Hospital Staff
Privileges:

November 1992 - Present
Edinburg Regional Medical Center
1102 West Trenton Rd
Edinburg, Texas 78539
Phone: 956-388-6000

November 1992 - Present
Edinburg Children's Hospital
1102 West Trenton Rd
Edinburg, Texas 78539
Phone: 956-388-6000

September 1997 - 2000
Mission Regional Medical Center
900 South Bryan Rd.
Mission, Texas 78572
956-580-9000

May 2000 - Present
Starr County Hospital
2753 Hospital Court
Rio Grande City, Texas 78582
956-487-5561

2010 - Present
Valley Baptist Medical Center Brownsville
1040 W. Jefferson
Brownsville, Texas 78520
956-698-5400

01/23/2007 - Present
Cornerstone Regional Hospital
2302 Cornerstone Blvd.

Mcallen, Texas 78503
956-618-4444

Lifecare Hospital of South Texas
5101 N Jackson Road
2001 S. M Street
Mcallen, Texas 78501
956-926-7093

Notes

1   Lila Watson, *Five Brothers in Four Countries* (*Five Brothers in Four Countries*, by Miss Lila Watson, a Southern Baptist missionary to China.) 89

2   Read the Niedens' story about their flight from eastern Siberia, through Harbin, Manchuria, to Shanghai, and subsequently to America, in the book titled, *Five Brothers in Four Countries*, by Miss Lila Watson, a Southern Baptist missionary to China.

Author:	Watson, Lila, 1892-1980
Other Authors:	Allan, Robert Tate.
Format:	Book
Language:	English
Published:	New York : Vantage Press, 1974
Edition:	1st ed.
Subjects:	Niedens family.
	Baptists > Biography.
	Christians > China.
	World War, 1939-1945 > Personal narratives, German.

Printed in the United States
By Bookmasters